HOW TO WRITE
Successful CVs and Job Applications

SECOND EDITION

JUDITH LEIGH

OXFORD
UNIVERSITY PRESS

Great Clarendon Street, Oxford, OX2 6DP,
United Kingdom

Oxford University press is a department of the University of Oxford.
It furthers the University's objective of excellence in research, scholarship, and education by publishing worldwide. Oxford is a registered trade mark of Oxford University press in the UK and in certain other countries

First published in 2004 as *CVs and Job Applications* in the One Step Ahead series
Second Edition 2013

Impression: 1

British Library Cataloguing in Publication Data
Data available

ISBN 978-0-19-967075-8

Printed in Great Britain by

Ashford Colour Press Ltd, Gosport, Hampshire

Contents

FAQs vi

Preface ix

Acknowledgements x

1 About this book 1

2 Groundwork 7

3 CVs 38

4 Covering letters 70

5 Job application forms 87

6 Online applications 100

7 Speculative applications 110

8 Interviews 120

9 Troubleshooting 137

Index 147

FAQs

What do I do if I don't know what sort of job I want?
Page 8

How do I know what skills I need for the job I want?
Page 111

What should I look for in an apprenticeship?
Page 117

What should a CV contain?
Page 38

How do I get experience?
Page 142

What if I want to change career?
Page 44, 73, 77, 144

Where do I look for jobs?
Page 26

What should a covering letter include?
Page 71

How can I improve my skills?
Page 20, 34

What if I've had a career break?
Page 44, 45, 72

Can I send my CV instead of filling in an application form?
Page 87

How do I turn interviews into job offers?
Page 137

How should I prepare for an interview?
Page 120

What do I do if there are no jobs locally?
Page 78, 142

What happens when I'm offered a job?
Page 134

How do I target a CV to a job?
Page 41

How can I find a job during a recession?
Page 140

Are CVs the same for all jobs?
Page 57

What should I do if my last job ended badly?
Page 129, 143

What is an application pack?
Page 16

For Richard S. Hopgood, with thanks for liking my CV.

Preface

In 2002, in the first edition of this book, I bravely forecast that the reader might come across the occasional online application. In a decade, the whole nature of the job search has changed. Online is in and paper is (almost) out. Websites are the places to find vacancies, not newspapers. You may well find that in a global marketplace, your boss is not just across the corridor, but across a continent and your interview is on Skype, not in a boardroom.

That said, the essential skills of the job hunt remain the same. The ability to write a CV, to explain in a limited number of written words why you are the ideal candidate and the way to present yourself at interview are still the key tasks of finding a job. In the current difficult economic circumstances, these are critical abilities, and this book will take you through how to acquire, improve, and revise them.

However challenging the financial climate makes the job market, there is plenty of help available on honing your job-seeking proficiency and tips on where to find this, and on how to create your own support network, and this is what this book provides.

Finally, this book aims to help you not just 'to get a job', but to find a career path that satisfies. If you, as I do, agree with Albert Camus, who said that 'without work, all life is rotten, but when work is soulless, life stifles and dies', then I hope that this book will enable you to find that extra dimension to employment that makes Monday mornings easy.

Judith Leigh
London 2013

Acknowledgements

This edition owes its existence to the support and wise help of Rebecca Lane and Jamie Crowther at Oxford University Press. My thanks to them for their advice and patience. I am also indebted to the friends and colleagues who took the time and trouble to share their experiences, especially Jackie Till, Eira Gibson, and Gill Ellis. My thanks also to Beth, Lola, Leon, Emili, Richard, and Chris for kindly sharing their CVs with me; to Eamee and Kate at The Reader Organisation for thoughts on apprenticeships.

About this book

1

CONTENTS

1
Introduction

1
Who is this book for?

2
Introducing four applicants

2
Using this book

6
The building blocks of the job hunt

Introduction

This book aims to help you get the job you want by telling the people you want to work with what they need to know.

This is the essence of what successful CVs and application forms are all about. They present the information that an employer needs to make a balanced judgement about your suitability for work with them. Although very few employers would offer you a job solely on the basis of your CV or application form, they are vital to gain you an interview. A badly presented or targeted CV or application will ensure that you never reach that stage.

This is a book of *guidelines* and although there are a few rules that everyone should follow—such as checking the spelling on a CV or application form—you will probably find a mix'n'match approach to its advice is best. Use the tips to find a basic system that works for you and develop this core system to suit your individual style and aspirations.

Get the job you want by telling the people you want to work with what they need to know.

Who is this book for?

First job, looking for a move up the career ladder, returning to work, changing direction: these are all key stages in working life. This book will take you through the steps you need to take to create CVs and write job applications to help you at these times.

A CV is not a static item that, once written, never needs revisiting. Similarly, the way you complete a job application form will change as your experience grows. For this reason, throughout the book, examples of CVs and job applications are given based on the experience of four people who are at different stages in their careers.

Introducing four applicants

Below are brief biographies of the four, one of which will hopefully equate roughly to your current career situation.

- *Joe* is 18 and has recently finished a BTECH, and is wondering how to start his career. He hasn't any strong feelings about which field to work in, other than the fact that he does not like a formal working environment and, in the future, he would like to be involved in creative work.
- *Kashmira* is in her late 20s and has been working for five years since graduating from university. She is beginning to feel bored in her current job and wants to make the first move into a management role. She isn't sure how to communicate her readiness to break into management from a junior post.
- *Hannah* is in her late 30s and has had a break from working while her children were young. Now that her children are all at school, she wants to get back to work. She had five years' work experience before she took her career break. Her last post was team supervisor in a call centre.
- *Richard* is in his early 50s. He has been working for the same company for the last ten years and has progressed through various roles to be currently the Design and Production Manager. Due to a planned merger, Richard knows his post will be made redundant in the next few months. He has decided to take a positive approach to this event as he feels this might be an ideal opportunity to change his career completely.

Using this book

The book follows the process of applying for a job as shown in the flow chart on pages 4–5. Each chapter starts with a general introduction to the topic covered followed by more specific descriptions and suggestions on the various points you will need to consider when building up your skills as a successful job applicant. The chapters conclude with a summary of the main hints and tips the chapter covers.

Chapter 2 deals with the preparation you need to do before you apply for any post. Chapters 3 to 7 deal with the different methods of applying for a job from CVs to online applications. Chapter 8 discusses interview techniques. Chapter 8 concludes with a brief overview of things you need to think about before confirming acceptance of a job, such as terms and conditions of employment. Chapter 9 is devoted to troubleshooting, giving hints and tips on common queries and problems when job hunting. This chapter also contains some hints about turning the situation round and making a fresh start when your career has run into difficulties.

Through the text, you will find

- *Quick Tips*: the 'do's and 'don't's of applying for a job.
- *Enhancing your skills*: suggestions on how to improve your work experience to build your career.
- *Making language work for you*: how to use language to raise your CV, application or covering letter to make a great presentation.

In the margins are a variety of quotations about work and finding a job. Some may make you smile, but if you find yourself in sympathy with too many of the negative views, perhaps it is time to plan a new strategy: either to your attitude to work or your approach to finding a job.

Flow chart of the job application process

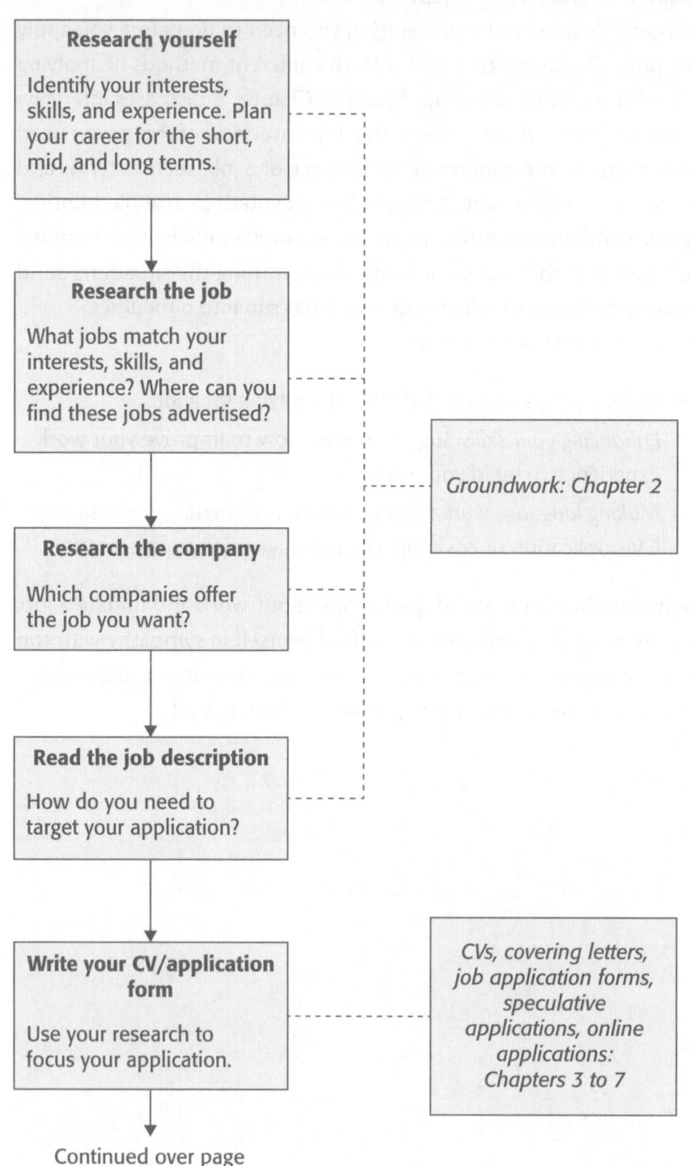

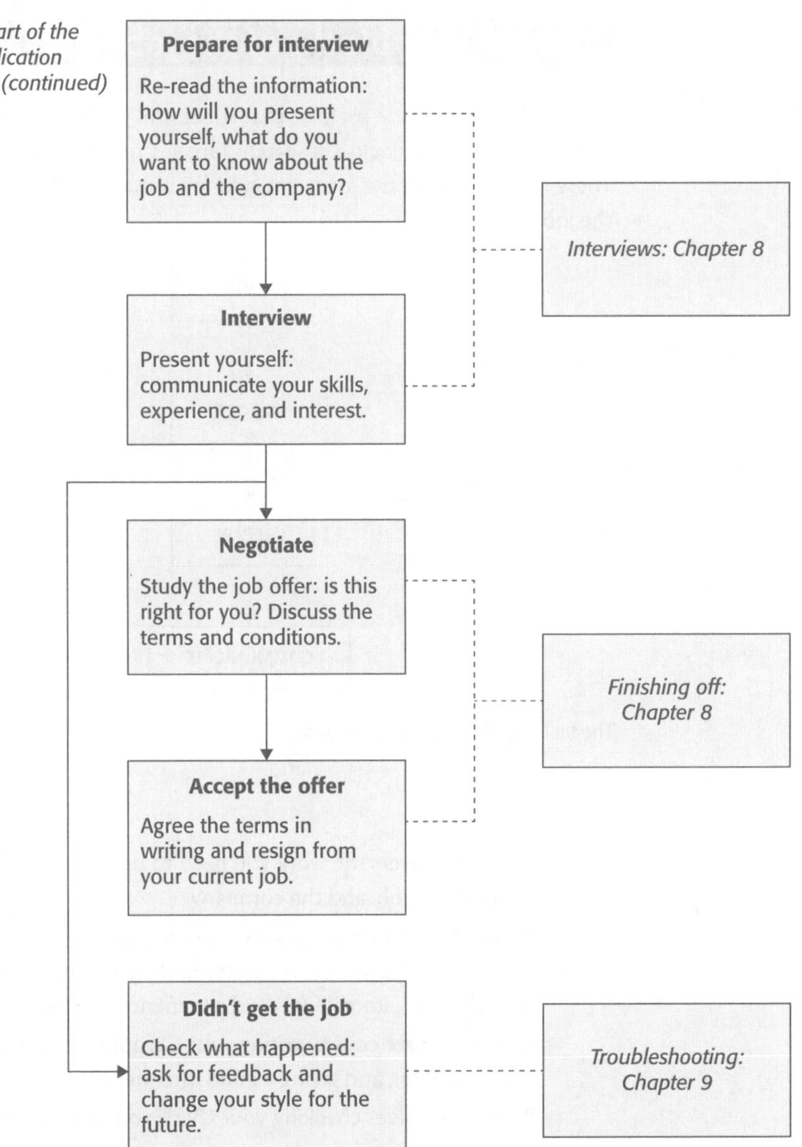

Flow chart of the job application process (continued)

The building blocks of the job hunt

This book works on the premise that successful job applications are built using four 'building blocks': Research, Target, Communicate and Prepare. These four blocks are the load, aim, and fire sequence which will land you the job you want.

The building blocks of job applications

- **Research** covers the work you need to do to find out about yourself, the job, and the company.
- **Target** means focusing your CV or job application to suit the demands of the job or conversely finding a company which best suits the skills, knowledge, and experience you have.
- **Communicate** covers writing your CV, application form, and covering letter, and giving a good interview.
- **Prepare** involves checking your CV or your application; practising for the interview.

Groundwork

2

CONTENTS

2
Researching yourself

16
Researching the job

31
Researching the company

35
Other groundwork

37
Summary of main points

A successful application is usually the result of good initial groundwork by the candidate. Taking time to work out what you want to do, what a job entails, and what makes an organization tick are some of the most important parts of a successful job hunt. Thinking back to the four building blocks outlined in Chapter 1, this groundwork includes the blocks of:

- Research
- Target
- Prepare

This chapter concentrates on the Research aspect of making a job application. Research is a vital part of any application and it falls into three parts:

- researching yourself
- researching the job you want to do
- researching the organization you want to work for

Researching yourself is a much bigger topic than can be covered in depth in this book. The first section of this chapter gives you pointers to get started but you will probably find it useful to look at other books dedicated to this area as well.

Researching jobs and organizations has never been easier thanks to the proliferation of information on the Internet, and guidelines to Internet searching are provided.

Throughout the chapter you will find hints and tips relating to improving your skills and chances in other areas of the job hunt or your career.

Being an MP is the sort of job all working-class parents want for their children—clean, indoors and no heavy lifting.
Diane Abbott, Independent

Best and worst aspects

- At solicitors' office, liked learning new things (the telephone switchboard was the best of all).
- Didn't like the very structured and formal atmosphere.
- At college, enjoyed the IT modules best.
- At college, liked the report-writing modules least.

Career aims

- Short term: to get a job!
- Mid term: don't know—being promoted?
- Long term: something creative?

Joe's responses are fairly typical for someone starting out: he has not had enough time to look round the job market and see what interests him or what parts of a job will be the best or most boring for him. Joe needs to try to find a job that ties into his interests but does not force him into a particular channel. When you start your working life, look for jobs which will give you:

- **core skills in the chosen broad area of your career**

  For example if you feel your career will be based in an office, look for an administrative post which will cover office basics such as computers, using a telephone system, and dealing with the public. If you are looking for a career in the catering trade, look for a post that will show you kitchen basics such as food preparation, hygiene, and use of different types of kitchen equipment.
- **opportunities for training**

  An ideal job goes on teaching you new things all the time, no matter where you are in your career. Companies which are not interested in promoting this aspect of work rarely have a good track record with their staff. Training may be structured, with day release or evening courses included (and sometimes even paid for), or on-the-job training with regular in-house sessions.

In a hierarchy every employee tends to rise to his level of incompetence.
Laurence J. Peter, The Peter Principle

- **a career structure**
  A sense of progression helps your motivation. Multinationals, the Civil Service, local Councils and academic institutions will have structured systems leading you up a career ladder (or crossing between different areas, say from retail to marketing). Smaller companies will have a looser structure, relying either on new work coming in to drive the process of promotion and job development, or on staff leaving and opening up opportunities for others. Which structure appeals to you will depend on your personality. However, look out for danger signs in firms where people seem to be 'stuck' in a role and are frustrated by this.

Quick Tip
There is nothing wrong in finding your 'niche' in a company and staying put at that level: HR managers are usually desperate to find stayers at all levels.

Joe has two or three 'ideal' careers open to him.

- Working as an administrator with a music company: an office job, but the atmosphere will be informal compared to that of a solicitors' office. There will be lots of different people to meet and Joe will have the opportunity to learn about the music industry from the bottom up.

- A post in a sports venue or in a company sponsoring sporting events. Posts do turn up with football clubs, but Joe would need more work experience before he could compete with the dozens of other applicants. It may be worth Joe's time contacting 'his' team and asking what qualifications and experience would be expected. Joe can then map a career and training which will fit him for the role. For example, if the club wants staff who have experience of particular software, Joe could look for companies who use this software or start saving to pay for private training in his spare time.

- A role with a company that has a creative aim; media, designers, architects, printers. Starting from scratch in a firm where training is encouraged and staff are promoted through experience would be helpful.

These are 'ideal' careers, but if Joe starts a flexible career plan now, with these jobs in mind, he will have a career direction. Being asked what your career plans are is a favourite interviewer's question, so having a plan now means you can present yourself much more dynamically on your CV and at interview.

The second example is Richard.

Quick Tip
Memberships of organizations demonstrate that you are actively involved in your interests and have made a certain commitment to supporting them.

Interests

- Countryside and the environment—member of the Ramblers, the National Trust, the Worldwide Fund for Nature, the Wildfowl & Wetlands Trust.
- Family—two daughters and one son (all in teens); occasional fostering for local authority.

Skills

Quick Tip

At this stage of your research, don't write detailed notes of every single skill you possess: do this section quickly so that the things you write down are the ones that immediately suggest themselves to you as your strongest skills.

- 20 years' experience in design and production; 10 years' management experience, including project management, costing and budget control, reporting to directors.
- Good verbal and written communication skills; experienced in writing and making presentations.
- Good at putting teams together and leading them.
- 8 O-levels, 3 A-levels, degree in Mechanical Engineering.

Quick Tip

Don't overlook your non-work talents. For example, in this exercise, Hannah's friends have all pointed out that she is wonderful with children. This 'skill' never occurred to Hannah because she doesn't see it as a work skill, but building on her ability could open up a whole new career as a teacher, play worker, self-employed childcare provider, counsellor…

Short-term career aims (now to 1 year)

- Depending on redundancy package, take training course in charity administration or fundraising with aim of finding job in charity which matches personal interests.

- Look for volunteering opportunities that could tie in with training timetable.

Mid-term career aims (1 year to 3 years)

- Having completed training, look for suitable post in a charity, and gain experience.

Long-term career aims (3 years onwards)

- Possibly move into political lobbying for charities

  Richard is, strangely enough, in a similar position to Joe. The end of his current job leaves him with a completely open field so that his career could go in a variety of directions. Where Richard differs from Joe is that he has a good idea of the sector he wants to work in: charity. Charities are interested in managers with solid experience and the range of skills Richard can demonstrate—his knowledge of production operations, his good communication skills in meetings and presentations. Richard also has a useful number of personal interests which demonstrate his commitment to a number of charities.

  Where Joe has the edge on Richard is that Richard's career has been in the same area for a long time which means he has things to 'unlearn'. For example, Richard may find it a shock to move back into a formal learning environment as he retrains and then moves from the commercial world into the charity sector. Out go the expense account lunches and annual bonuses: in come stringent financial restraints and a hands-on approach to all aspects of a job. Before setting off on his chosen course, Richard would need to consider:

- **Finances**

  It is essential when switching careers to be prepared for your salary to plummet in the short term and work out how you will cover the shortfall. Exactly how much do you need to live on and, from this, what salary must you earn?

- **Training**

  What courses will give you the knowledge you need? What do they cost, where are they run, and when do they start? Do you need a minimum qualification to join? What qualification do you gain at the end and is this the qualification linked to the job you have in mind? It is essential to plan your training to fit in with the rest of your game plan: having a vague idea about retraining will be a disaster if you find out that you missed the starting date of the only course by a month and have to wait a year before it starts again.

- **having a 'taster'**

  If, like Richard, you have never worked in a charity, it would be worth having a trial before you switch careers. Charities are usually delighted to have volunteers, though it is likely that voluntary work will be of a lower grade than you might be used to—anything from stuffing envelopes to hacking down undergrowth. Similarly, if you want to change roles in business, use your contacts inside and outside your current company, friends and relatives, to see if you can 'shadow' someone in the job you are interested in for a few days. Learning what it is like from the inside can be an eye-opener.

What's missing?

After you have thought through the key questions, it is worth getting a second opinion on your answers. Both Joe and Richard have missed important parts out of their personal profiling: Joe has not listed his BTECH under *Skills and experience*; Richard has forgotten that he has committed himself to a sponsored cycle ride for one month in his *Short-term career aims*. Another view of each of their situations would have been very helpful.

Ask a family member, a trusted friend, or work colleague to write their own list of what they think your strengths and weaknesses are. It is best if they do this quite quickly—ask them to spend no more than ten minutes writing single words under the headings *Strengths* and *Weaknesses*. This way you will get a more honest response, but this is why it is important that you do this exercise with someone you trust. Work colleagues must be reliable enough not to share their views and your intentions to change jobs with the rest of the company. If you know someone who is in a similar situation to you, this could be a mutually useful exercise. If Richard knows another manager in a different department who is also expecting to be made redundant, then they could work together on this project.

You could be very surprised at the feedback you gain. For example, Joe's best friend puts the word 'shy' under Joe's weaknesses, although Joe thinks that he gets on well with people. Joe gets on well with *friends*, but he tends to be shy when he meets people face-to-face—hence his enjoyment of switchboard work at the solicitors. Joe will need to spend some time debating if he should work on this weakness or look for a job where he has less contact with strangers.

Richard's wife has reminded him that he did do some voluntary work about ten years ago: it would be interesting for Richard to work out why he had forgotten about this. Was it very boring or did he have so much fun that it didn't feel like work?

A totally independent view can also be beneficial. Don't forget to make use of your local careers advisory service. Universities often offer their own graduates free careers advice, plus workshops on interviewing skills and CV writing. Large companies implementing a redundancy programme will also usually offer employees sessions with external consultants.

If you are at managerial level, consider using a dedicated consultancy. These are not recruitment consultancies and work in a quite different way, analysing your career aspirations and experience in rigorous detail and coaching you on a one-to-one basis to improve your interviewing and presentation skills. Such consultancies frequently have access to unadvertised jobs and will actively look for appropriate posts for you. However, they are expensive: you will probably have to pay a fee and if the agency places you in a job, you may have to agree to pay the agency a percentage of your first year's salary. You must therefore make your own careful investigation of the integrity and track record of the company you select.

A word of caution

Self-research can be quite painful on occasion. You will find most respected self-help books will advise you that this can be an exhausting process which can throw up all sorts of long forgotten troubles and angsts. Take the process slowly and if you decide to seek outside help, look for a counsellor with the relevant qualifications from a recognized body. Companies offering psychometric testing–a form of aptitude, ability, and career development testing–should be registered with the British Psychological Society, www.bps.org.uk.

Reviewing your plan

It is important to give yourself a time frame, and revisit your plan regularly (perhaps every two months if you are out of work, and every six months if you are in work) to alter it as circumstances change. Your plan is not set in stone, but giving yourself some deadlines can help motivate you to achieve it. At the same time, don't be tempted into *constantly* revisiting it and worrying that you are not where you expected to be: this demotivates and breeds a sense of failure. Congratulate yourself when you achieve a step: revise the plan when you find the step is not achievable.

Researching the job

What's in a name?

A rose by any other name would smell as sweet...

William Shakespeare

When you read through job adverts, the purpose of some jobs seems obvious—a PA, a baker, a police officer, a teacher are all instantly recognizable roles. But what about a communications administrator, an archaeology commissions manager, or an SRB5 project officer? There are also roles which have different meanings to different companies: distributions manager, site manager, director. The fact is that all roles, even the seemingly straightforward ones such as baker and teacher, are unique.

This is why many job advertisements carry the crucial phrase 'full job description available' or 'call for application pack'. It may be tempting to fire off your CV to a company as soon as you have read the advert, but the opportunity is being handed to you on a plate to find out what the job really entails. Without doing so, you will probably find later that you applied incorrectly: either because you would not have been interested in the job if you knew what it involved or because you failed to target your application appropriately.

Comprehensive application packs will consist of:

- job description
- person specification

- company information
- department information
- information about the recruitment procedure
- information about the terms and conditions of employment
- application form

The *job description* will tell you what the responsibilities and tasks are that make up the job. As a general rule, the shorter and simpler the description, the less responsibility the post has in a company hierarchy. Descriptions of management posts may run to several pages and include details of targets or policy to be implemented.

A *person specification* describes the organization's perfect candidate. It may be divided into qualifications, skills, and work experience, and these sections will be subdivided into 'essential' and 'desirable'. Essential items are those you must have; desirable items will give you an additional edge.

As you read through the job description and person specification, make notes for yourself, identifying:

- the tasks you already have skills and experience in. You will need to highlight these in your CV or on the application form.
- the tasks you have never tried before and whether these are of interest to you. What case can you make in your covering letter for being able to do these (e.g. being a quick learner, this is the area you want to move into)?
- questions about the company such as what its primary business is and how big it is, how many people work there.
- questions about the team you will be working in: how big is it, what is its primary role in supporting the business, who you report to.
- anything you can read between the lines: are there unexpected tasks in this role or an emphasis on certain skills? Emphasis, for example, on managing client relations in the description of a job which does not appear to be primarily about client relations may indicate the company is in trouble in this area. If a person specification concentrates on skills and experience at working with a 'hard-pressed' team you may deduce that the team has had difficulties or awkward people are involved. Think what you could do to bring a fresh eye and experience in resolving these.

Quick Tip

Keep copies of person specifications of jobs you would have liked to apply for or companies you would have liked to work for if you had had all the essential items listed. Use these as guidelines for future career development: how can you mould your career to give you these skills or experience?

Job title	Sales Support Administrator
Overall purpose of job	• to provide efficient and effective support administration to the sales team
Responsibilities	• handling phone calls, letters, and email from existing and potential clients; logging correspondence on the database and diarying for follow up • setting up meetings for the sales team; arranging any travel and accommodation required • receiving debriefs from the sales team and logging these on the system for follow up • drawing up sales contracts for dispatch to clients; chasing up; checking when received and entering on system • liaising with Finance Department to send out invoices • liaising with Distribution Department to ensure right product is sent to right customer on date promised • logging commission due to each of sales team and producing monthly report • making courtesy follow-up calls to customers to check products received and working correctly • attending sales meetings and taking notes • helping train new sales staff in procedures used • any other duties as required

Notes on the left:

- How big is the team? How many reps? How many administrators? (→ overall purpose of job)
- How many clients are there? How many leads does the sales team get annually/monthly /weekly? (→ handling phone calls, letters, and email)
- Business travel not something I've done before: what other experience can I use to show I can do this? (→ setting up meetings)
- Lots of data entry work: what system do they use? (→ receiving debriefs)
- Sounds like this has been a problem in the past: how can I improve the situation? (→ liaising with Distribution Department)
- Good! I like training aspect! (→ helping train new sales staff)

Notes on the right:

- Yes, all done before and I have been complimented by manager on how I handle clients (→ handling phone calls, letters, and email)
- I've arranged holidays and trips for myself (→ setting up meetings)
- I've carried out liaison before and I think it's one of my strengths because I build relationships with colleagues (→ liaising with Finance Department; liaising with Distribution Department)
- This would be new: but I take notes all the time as customers are giving orders and it's a good chance to understand more of what the sales team are doing (→ attending sales meetings and taking notes)

Example of a job description with notes

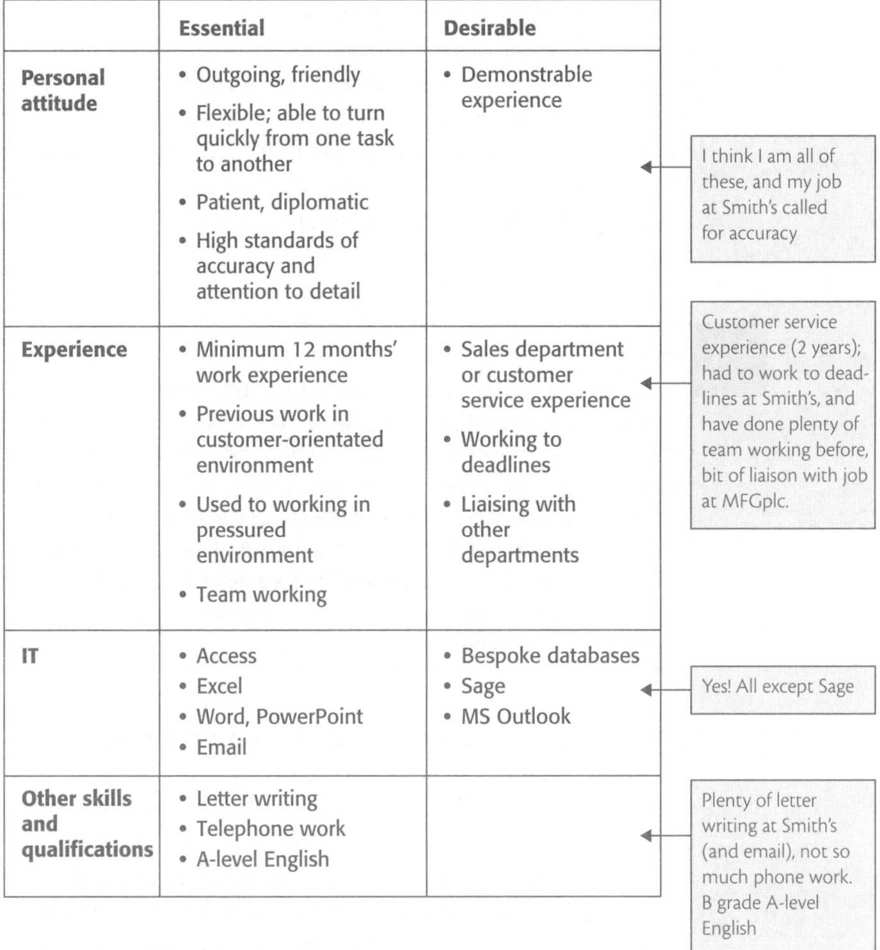

	Essential	Desirable
Personal attitude	• Outgoing, friendly • Flexible; able to turn quickly from one task to another • Patient, diplomatic • High standards of accuracy and attention to detail	• Demonstrable experience
Experience	• Minimum 12 months' work experience • Previous work in customer-orientated environment • Used to working in pressured environment • Team working	• Sales department or customer service experience • Working to deadlines • Liaising with other departments
IT	• Access • Excel • Word, PowerPoint • Email	• Bespoke databases • Sage • MS Outlook
Other skills and qualifications	• Letter writing • Telephone work • A-level English	

Example of a person specification with notes

Company and department information will give you a notion of what the company's immediate and long-term aims are and how the department fits into this plan. Again, look for the hidden clues. 'After a period of change, the department is now aiming to provide its users with high standards of service' means that staff morale may be very low following a serious shake up, or may be very high thanks to a dynamic manager who has revived a stagnant department. Look for other clues to decide which is the correct solution: has this vacancy come about as the result of a promotion or someone leaving? What does the organizational information tell you? Has there been anything about this company in the news lately? Check out the Internet, not confining your search only to the company's website, but look for stories in the local or national press, customer feedback on blogs and sales sites.

Enhancing your skills

If you are looking for your first move into management, one way you could increase your knowledge of good (and bad) organizational practices is by taking an active role in local charities or membership of professional organizations to which you belong. Charities are often in search of people willing to serve as trustees and it's an excellent way to make a difference to the charity – and to your career plans. One charity in Gloucester recruits trustees from students of the Business Management course of its local university: the charity gains the benefit of the latest business thinking, and the students gain hands on experience of strategic management and a very useful item to add to their CVs.

The details on *recruitment procedure* will also give some hints on the role. Everyone expects to be interviewed for a job, but the procedure may also involve going to an assessment centre for a day of tests, group exercises, and panel interviews. Don't be put off by such procedures; they are typical for fast track executive or senior management roles and if you have the chance, try the system once at least. Graduate entry schemes might include an open day, where you have the chance to quiz existing staff and get a general feel for what it is like to work at the company. Seize every chance you get to go to these as they will all increase your knowledge of a sector and the skills you need to succeed in it.

Terms and conditions will tell you the salary and benefits of the job. Everyone wants to know what they will be paid, but take a moment to look at what else might be on offer. A lower salary might be offset by generous holiday leave, free childcare, opportunities for paid study leave or subsidized mortgages. Most employers only supply 'full terms and conditions' when a job offer is made (covering items like actual starting and finishing times, probationary period, and sick leave) but you might want to make a note to ask anything you are especially keen to know if you get an interview. At this point, you need to check that what is being offered suits you.

The language of job adverts

Below are explanations of various abbreviations and expressions commonly used in job adverts.

- **a.e.:** according to experience. Used in conjunction with salary details, for example £12,000–£14,000 a.e., meaning that the salary offered to you would depend on your previous relevant experience.
- **application pack:** a pack containing information on an advertised job, usually consisting of a job description, a person specification, information on the organization, recruitment procedures that will be used, terms of employment including salary, benefits, hours of work, and holidays.
- **circa**, as in *salary circa £20,000*: in the region of. The company will be offering a salary around the £20,000 mark. A rule of thumb is that the salary will be somewhere between £1,000 below and £2,000 above the stated figure.
- **covering letter:** a letter to be sent with a CV or application form, setting out in detail why you are applying for the job. A common mistake is to send a letter which purely states, in effect, 'here is my CV'. This is not what the employer wants: you need to pick out the relevant parts of your CV for the role and why you think you are suitable. If you are responding to an advertised post, check what length of letter the employer expects (usually no more than two sides of A4). If you are sending a speculative letter and CV to an employer you would like to work for, your covering letter should be no more than one side of A4.
- **FAO:** For the Attention Of in the context of 'mark your application FAO Fiona Smith, HR Department'.
- **f/t** or **F/T:** full time. Jobs classed as 'full time' require you to work for between 35 hours and 40 hours per week. The hours may be spread over five × eight-hour days, or may take the form of longer shifts over shorter days.
- **fixed term:** these are jobs which have a definite ending date, rather than a permanent job which has no end date and theoretically could run until the employee retires. Fixed-term contract jobs are often involved with projects which run for a predetermined length of time. Companies may also use fixed-term contracts when they are not sure if they can afford to pay for another permanent member of staff, but want to test

Quick Tip

The salary quoted in adverts is almost always gross, before the deduction of tax and insurance contributions. Take this into account when calculating what salary you need to cover living expenses.

out how beneficial the job (and the jobholder) is to the company. If your job falls into the latter category, you need continuously to prove yourself indispensable so that the post becomes permanent.

- **flexitime:** flexitime covers a system of working whereby you undertake to work for a given number of hours a week or month, but determine what time you start and finish each day. You may be required to be present for **core hours**, such as 10 a.m. to 3 p.m., when the office expects to be at its busiest. Flexitime may also mean that there is no overtime: if you do more hours than required, you take time off in lieu of payment. Check which flexitime system the employer operates, and especially what the core hours are, if you have personal commitments at certain times of the day.
- **hinterland:** your personal interests and hobbies are your 'hinterland' on a CV or job application, providing the recruiter with an opportunity to perceive you as a fully rounded person, with a life outside work.
- **hpw:** hours per week. Used in the sense '35 hpw, Mondays to Fridays'.
- **HR:** Human Resources. This is the modern term for Personnel, and means rather more. Personnel tends to concern the basics of employment such as salaries and terms and conditions. HR looks beyond the small details to understanding that people are a company's most important and valuable asset, and planning how to use this 'resource' to the company's best benefit. HR is involved with whole strategies, contributing to every part of an organization's needs and aims.
- **job share:** job sharing means the sharing of a single job between two or more people who work at different times. It is very popular with employees who wish to spend more time with their family, or have other personal interests to pursue. To job share successfully, you need:
  - to know your job partner well and get on with them;
  - to be able to communicate with each other to a very high standard;
  - to work in the same style, as you must be able to pick up exactly where the other person left off.
- Job sharing used to be confined to higher management and professional posts, such as those of solicitors. However, job sharing is now becoming more frequent at every level. If you have a friend with whom you would like to job share, it is worth writing joint applications to see if an employer is interested.

  Job sharing is a good way to get back into work if you have had time out to raise a family, or after illness. Hannah and her friend Carrie have reached an informal arrangement that if they can find a job share post, each of them will look after the other's children as well as their own on two days a week. On the fifth day, when both may be required to be in the office, they will use a childcare agency.

- **k:** thousand, so £18k = £18,000.
- **LW** or **LWA:** London Weighting or London Weighting Allowance. Because of the higher costs of living, an additional amount may be paid by companies operating across the UK or other organizations (such as the emergency services) which have a national pay structure. Outer and Inner London weighting may also be paid, reflecting the fact that costs get progressively higher the closer in to London you work. Note that you do not have to be living in London to qualify for this extra amount: it is the job which attracts the weighting.
- **no agencies:** the company advertising the job will not accept applications sent by recruitment agencies, as the company does not wish to pay agency fees. Useful to know if you are registered with one or more agencies as your CV will definitely not have been sent to the advertiser.
- **OTE:** On Target Earnings. Sales and promotional jobs often have quite a small basic salary while the rest is made up of commission. The OTE figure tells you more than how much you might make if you are good at the job, it is also the amount the company *expects* you to make. Check carefully how the commission is calculated to gain an idea of how much business you must do, and decide if you are capable of handling the work and pressure involved in reaching that target.
- **p.a.:** per annum, literally 'for the year'. Used in conjunction with a salary to show the amount you will be paid in each calendar year, for example £14,000 p.a.
- **PA:** Personal Assistant. A senior administrative job, usually providing support to one person or a small team. Often described as being the 'right-hand person' type of role, to show the depth of reliance placed on the jobholder.
- **PR:** Public Relations. PR is the presentation of a company to the outside world and generally refers to relations with clients and the press. However, the organization may also include marketing, communicating with internal departments, and any other form of contact with staff and clients under this catch-all title.
- **PRP:** Performance Related Pay. PRP ties in salary to the individual employee's performance and/or the performance of the team, department, or company as a whole over a set period. Employees are paid a basic salary, and then a bonus depending on whether targets are

met in full or in part. PRP structures can be very rewarding for hard work, but can also be complicated with many built-in provisos, so ensure that you understand the scheme before signing up to it.

- **pro rata:** literally 'according to the rate'. Used in conjunction with salary where the job is part time or for a fixed term of less than a calendar year. The salary will be given as, for example, '£20,000 per annum pro rata'. This means that if you were doing the job full time, or for a full year, the salary would be £20,000, but it will be reduced in proportion to the hours or length of your job. Thus if you worked for four days a week, the salary would be reduced by a fifth to £16,000 or if your job lasted for six months, you would be paid a total of £10,000 in that time.
- **p/t** or **P/T:** part time. Where a job is for fewer hours or days than the organization's standard hours or days, it is part time. The job still counts as being permanent. You are entitled to receive the same benefits as full-time workers, adjusted where appropriate for the smaller number of hours or the lower salary.
- **s/h:** shorthand. It is applied to secretarial posts which require the jobholder to be able to take shorthand dictation.
- **SME:** Small and Medium Enterprises; refers to business organizations with fewer than 500 staff. There are now a considerable number of jobs in the market which deal with the promotion of or giving assistance to SMEs, as part of local or national business initiatives. You will need to have a good grasp of the issues faced by SMEs, preferably from first-hand experience, if you are attracted by such roles.
- **working knowledge:** this means your knowledge of a skill (for example, of a software program) should be sufficient for you to use it easily in a job, though you may not have had formal training in it.
- **WPM:** Words Per Minute. Used in relation to the speed at which you must be able to type (60 wpm) or at which you can take shorthand dictation (100 wpm). To see how fast you are, type a page or pages from a book for exactly five minutes on a word processor. Then count the words you have typed (most word-processing packages can do this for you) and divide by five to get your minute rate. To check shorthand speed, use the same passage you have typed and ask a friend or relative to read it out while you take it down in shorthand, again for five minutes. Your rate will be slightly faster as you already know the passage, so deduct 10 per cent from your final figure.

Making language work for you: the language of employers

Just as a recruitment manager can read your CV and pick up on the clues you have given them (whether consciously or unconsciously) an advert for a job or an application pack can give you all sorts of pointers–if you know how to read them.

Apart from the acknowledged jargon that adverts use, the way the advert is written shows the style of the company. See below for two adverts for very similar posts but they are streets apart in the techniques they are using to attract candidates. Example A shows a conventional advert, Example B a more dynamic method. If you decided to apply for both jobs, you would be justified in taking a more informal and proactive approach in your application to Example B on the evidence of the advert alone. However, neither advert gives very much information and you would need to do more research on both organizations before beginning to write an application that was well focused and would be interesting to the recruiter. You will find more about how to research a company in a later section of this chapter.

Keeping a file of adverts which have interesting, different, or useful descriptions of skills and tasks can be helpful in building up your vocabulary. Do not look just for adverts in your chosen area; check out adverts for everything from education to IT and see what language they use too. Many skills and tasks are common to a whole range of jobs. Using a description from a different career sector can often be effective in catching the eye of a recruitment manager who has become bored with standard descriptions, but take care not to give the impression that you have no knowledge of the jargon of your chosen career sector.

Example A

Poetry in Schools Administrator

£15,000–£18,000 p.a.

The Poetry in Schools Project, set up in 2005, supports five poets in residence at various schools in Lancashire, and arranges visits to schools by poets.

An administrator is required to assist the Manager with all aspects of the Project. You will need to be fully IT literate and have experience of working with teachers. Events administration would be advantageous.

Hours Mon–Fri, 9–5 p.m. Some travelling will be necessary. This post is graded as AO Level 2 under the LGO guidelines with 20 days leave and appropriate pension package.

Example B

Do You Know your Hughes from Your Heaney?

Poetry Officer

£15,000–£18,000 p.a.

Poetry North West is seeking a poetry enthusiast to help set up a new poet in residence scheme with local businesses. You'll need to have plenty of energy, arranging and attending meetings with the Project Manager, liaising with poets and helping to publicize the scheme. Obviously you'll be IT literate, thrive on a challenge, and ideally have some press experience.

Interested? If so, send your CV and a covering letter to...

Terms and conditions of employment are dealt with in Chapter 8.

Where to look

Researching a job you have already spotted being advertised is easy: what about finding a job to research to start with?

THE INTERNET

The big change in the job market over the last 10 years has been the role the Internet has in advertising job vacancies. It is now the biggest marketplace for employers looking for staff. The trick is how to focus your search and not be daunted by the plethora of entries that appear when you enter 'job vacancies' into a search engine.

Narrow your search terms by thinking in terms of:

- the job title (but remember that job titles can mean different things in different organizations).
- the sector you want to work in.
- the geographical location where you want to work.

The website address of a company can often tell you which country the company is based in. The suffix.uk will tell you this is a UK-based company, the suffix .au is for Australia, .nz for New Zealand. This means you can save time by ignoring those search results for companies based outside the country you wish to work in.

Internet searching is a delicate balance between being so definite in your search terms that you find nothing, and being so broad in your search terms that you find too much. It's generally easiest to start with a narrowly focused search and try gradually widening it out. If you have developed a specially good search string, keep a note of it for future re-use, rather than having to re-invent it.

> Joe started by typing in 'sports vacancies' to a search engine and found over 47 million hits. After a think, he tried instead 'sports administrator vacancies birmingham' (which reduced the number of hits to 16.5 million) and found several websites which concentrate on football posts, one of which was advertising an apprenticeship administrator role with a West Midlands club. The problem was the post was not in Joe's home town of Birmingham, but he checked the details and found there was a possibility of subsidized travel through a government scheme and a frequent train service. This would be a good career starter for Joe, so it is worth investing in the travel aspect to gain the experience and skills he needs.

Internet vacancies are advertised by:

- *general recruitment sites*, such as Monster, Jobsite, fish4jobs, TheLadders, FreshMinds, which carry adverts from a whole range of companies and organizations. Some offer the opportunity to register your CV on the site so that employers looking for people with your skills, experience, and qualifications will be sent your CV when a match crops up. Others will match key words in your CV to key words in adverts and send you a regular email listing vacancies. Before you do register your details, do have a look at the sorts of jobs which the site advertises: some are aimed specifically at entry level, others at graduates, others at senior level management roles. Once you feel the roles being advertised are the right type for you, look at the wording in the adverts which interest you most and make sure these key words are included in your registration with the site.
- *recruitment agencies' sites*, such as Reed or Adecco. These companies have specialties in regard to sector (such as insurance, catering, automotive) or entry level (graduate, manager) or

geographic area. Again, besides giving you the opportunity to scan current opportunities, these sites allow you to register your CV and receive automatic emails when a new job comes up which matches your profile.

Recruitment agencies

Recruitment agencies divide roughly into two halves:

- those which deal with jobs from very junior positions up to lower management level in one or more sectors. At these agencies, you register with the agency and they will check your skills and experience against jobs on their register to find a match. Registering with an agency will give you the opportunity to hear about jobs which are not advertised elsewhere. The better agencies will be keen to help you achieve your career aims and will take the time to give you advice and guidance: listen to it.
- those which deal with middle and senior management posts. These consultancies have well-established relations with a number of companies or are known for finding and placing a certain type of manager in a given sector. They do not have a registration system for candidates and work on the basis of advertising in the press and sometimes on their website. Applications are then filtered by the agency before being passed to the company they have been retained by. These consultancies also headhunt, by knowing the senior or specialized personnel at companies in their field. They will approach someone who they think fits a profile and will open negotiations with them. Once a consultancy finds you a post, they will often remain in contact with you and be open to approaches when you are looking for a new post.

The golden rule when job searching with an agency is to ensure that the agency knows what type of job you want and what your skills and experience are. You can achieve this by filling in any registration forms honestly and building up a relationship with your consultant by giving feedback after each interview the agency arranges for you. This avoids you attending interviews which are not suitable. Irrelevant interviews are irritating for you, the agency, and the employer.

If the agency persists in sending you details of inappropriate jobs, you need to explain this to them and if this brings no results, ask to be taken off their books.

QUICK TIP

Keep a note of the name and contact details of agencies that seem to be advertising the type of jobs you are interested in. Visit the agency's website and if the majority of jobs are roughly in your area of interest, register your profile with the agency.

- *company websites*: many companies advertise their own vacancies on their websites. These pages will also give you vital data about what information the company needs from you to consider your application. If a company states that it is not currently considering applications, respect this and do not waste your time or the company's by sending speculative applications. Very large organizations will also have a regular email with vacancies or post vacancies at a given date each month.

  It may seem these sites are only useful if you know which company you are interested in working for and can search for its website directly. However, remember that doing an Internet search on the area of business you are interested in will produce lists of companies which work in that field. For example, if you are interested in being a sales rep in the electrical industry, a search on the key words 'electrical sales' will produce a list of companies selling electrical goods. If your search produces a daunting result list of thousands of entries, narrow your search by adding additional words such as 'jobs', 'careers', or 'opportunities'. You can also focus your search by geographical area, by adding, say, 'north east' or 'Bedfordshire' to 'electrical sales'.
- *national and local news sites*: although you can still buy the print version of national papers, it is now cheaper and quicker to use their websites to search for jobs. Local papers will have a variety of jobs, while the national papers tend to have their specialties:
  - *Guardian*: jobs at all levels in the media, arts and museums, social services, education, local government, charities, IT, and a general section dedicated to a raft of unusual and blue chip companies. Good career guide section also carried, with descriptions of jobs, what qualifications and experience they require, details of companies, and their 'rating' as a place of employment.
  - *Times*: posts at all levels of graduate entry, executive and higher management in blue chip companies, charities, local and national government, health service, law. Selection of experienced and junior administration and secretarial posts. Also publishes the *Times Educational Supplement* which covers educational and teaching posts.

- *Daily Telegraph*: particularly strong in engineering and operational management posts.

QUICK TIP
If you're not sure what trade publications there are for the area you want to look for a job in, ask your local reference library, as libraries have comprehensive catalogues of all available publications.

- *trade and sector publication sites*: most sectors have their own regular publications which are now available online. Publications which cover their sector as a whole (such as *Third Sector* for the charity/not for profit world and *The Grocer* for the food and drink industry) also carry job adverts. Some are free sites and others are subscription sites. In the case of the latter, look for offers of one free download before investing in an annual subscription. It can be worth taking a broad view of the sector such sites cover: for example, as well as industry-specific roles, *The Grocer* has jobs in logistics and operations, which could be interesting to you even if you have never thought about the food industry as a career.
- *social/professional networks*: you can use these networks in two ways. First, by linking to the pages of companies in which you are interested you can keep an eye on developments which might mean there will be vacancies in the future. Second, use your own network page to advertise your availability and ask friends to keep an eye out for you. Professional associations and niche market specialists are increasingly using networks such as LinkedIn to advertise opportunities, so even if you are not connected to their page, other friends who are linked can pass on details to you.

Be prepared to take your time over a productive Internet search. Ideally, do not combine it with registering for jobs: do your research in one phase, and your application registration in another phase, so that the Research block does not get muddled with the Communicate block.

OTHER SOURCES TO CONSIDER

Jobcentres: your local Jobcentre will have listings of local jobs as well as careers advice. If you have been out of work for a while, the Jobcentre may signpost you to local community services which run job clubs. These are definitely worth joining as they will motivate you, give you the chance to mix with other people in a similar situation, and the opportunity to take training courses in essential job hunt skills (such as interviewing) and to improve your work skills. Job clubs also offer free access to the Internet and often free phone calls to make appointments for interviews.

Local jobs are still often advertised by notices in windows of shops and offices so taking a walk along your local high street or around your local business estate can be profitable.

Free magazines and newspapers are usually paid for by their advertisers, and often have a wide range of vacancies at entry level.

Networking to find job vacancies is a long-established procedure and carries good and bad connotations. The concept of it not being what you know but who you know that gets you the job can be very frustrating, if you feel you are not part of the 'right' network. What you need to remember is that you have your own network which starts with family, then friends, then past and present colleagues. A few phone calls or an email to everyone you know asking them to keep an eye out for openings often produces unexpected returns. As you rise up the career ladder, your network should get bigger and perhaps more specialized as your career settles into one area. This is why senior managers get headhunted from one company to another: they have been dealing and working with similar—perhaps even the same—people for long enough for their reputation and skills in a certain area to be well known and attractive to another company. Forget the 'old school tie' network: any reputable company has scrapped this recruitment principle years ago. A word of warning though: think twice about working with or for someone you know as a friend. While they may be great company for a night out, do you really want to work day in and day out with that person?

Researching the company

The final part of your programme of research is to find out about the company (or any type of organization) to which you want to apply.

If you have received an application pack from a company, this is the stage where you need to consider the company information sent with the pack. Such information may consist of:

- a **publicity leaflet**: only useful up to a certain extent because it is aimed at customers and will give a limited number of facts.

- a mission **statement**: a short statement of the company's aims and aspirations, which may also give a breakdown of the current situation of the company and future targets.
- information on the **company structure**: often given in the form of departmental diagrams showing the management structure. From these diagrams you should be able to deduce if this is an organization with a loose, flat structure where most employees have the chance to make direct contributions to the strategy and operation of the company. Alternatively, there may be a more rigid, hierarchical structure with layers of staff at different grades. You need to go back to the research on yourself and decide which structure will best suit your preferred style of working.
- **annual reports and accounts**: the crucial parts of the report and accounts to look at are the chairperson's statement, the balance sheet, and the profit and loss account. The chair's statement will give you valuable hints about what the company has achieved over the past twelve months and what is intended for the next year. Have any weaknesses been identified or are performance strengths being built on? Do not be automatically deterred by a statement which refers to redundancies or cutting back *as long as it has already happened*: companies which have already taken action to resolve problems are in a stronger position than a company which has a vague statement from the chair about possible future restructuring. In the accounts, compare the figures for the current year to the previous year (which will also be in the accounts). Does the chair's statement explain major differences? If there has been a big jump in realizing capital assets, this may be a warning that the company is having to raise money to cover lost customers. However, it could also be to finance the purchase of new technology or investment in new areas: either way, the chair's statement should explain this.

!

Quick Tip

The further you progress up the career ladder, the more important a careful examination of the annual report and accounts becomes. You may be expected to give your appraisal at interview of the company's financial situation and how you can contribute to it. Your benefits package may consist of shares in the company: check that they are worth the paper they are written on before accepting.

- **latest newsletter**: again, if this is a newsletter for customers (this includes members of a membership organization), it will give you the positive aspects of a company and you need to be wary of accepting it fully at face value. However, the fact that an organization cares enough for its customers to keep them updated should give it extra marks.

Larger organizations often have a staff newsletter as well as a customer newsletter. This can be useful in giving you a feel for the 'culture' of the company: does it concentrate on sales targets or stories about how well the staff football team did?

Quick Tip

Make notes for yourself as you read through company information. What are the key factors that should be included in your application? Is there anything that is not fully explained which could be discussed at interview?

Stay informed

Retain the application pack a company sends you. If you are invited to an interview, re-reading this information will form part of your interview preparation (***see*** Chapter 9). You will find it annoying if you are invited to interview only to discover you no longer have the company information and the recruitment manager will not be impressed if you ask for it again.

If you are not invited to interview or are not offered the job after an interview but are still interested in the company, keep the pack for future applications. It would be interesting to compare what the company sends out in six months' or a year's time, and will gain you marks at interview if you can demonstrate an ongoing interest in and knowledge of the company. Think of setting up a quick reference system which focuses on key points such as the names of managers, products, income, number of customers (or members), any plans for expansion or new ventures.

Do-it-yourself research

If the company does not send you any information, you will need to do some research yourself.

- **Check the company website**

  This will give you a company overview and other clues. For example, what sort of website is it? An attractive, well-planned site speaks volumes, as much as a plain or dull site does. Is company news on the website up to date, or is the last entry six months old or more? If the former, this is a company which understands the importance of digital media; if the latter, is there a chance for you to flag your interest and/or experience in this area?

Enhancing your skills

Taking responsibility in a small organization for the website is a good way to expand your hard and soft skills. Besides the technical side of uploading information and perhaps even website design, it can involve liaising with different colleagues to understand what they want a website to do for them; gathering information on products, company news, sector news and writing and putting it into an appropriate format; monitoring use of the website and thinking how this usage can be enhanced and improved. Our job hunter, Kashmira (***see*** Chapter 1) realized she was ready to make her first move into management when she took charge of overhauling the company's website, liaising with the contractor who provided it, presenting new designs, setting up regular meetings with the management team to add new information and finding the company's web sales had risen by 150%.

- **Ask the company**

  Applicants are sometimes reluctant to ask the company itself for more details in case they appear ignorant. It would be very unusual for any recruitment manager to think this and much more likely for them to be immediately interested in a candidate who shows initiative.
- **Ask the agency**

  If you are being sent on an interview by a recruitment agency, they should be able to brief you properly about both the post *and* the company and may be able to find out more if you have special queries.
- **Ask those in the know**

  If you know anyone working at the company, you will get an insider's view. You can also ask around your network to see, first, if they know the company or, second, if they know anyone who knows the company well. They may know the general field the company works in and the reputation the company has.

- **Recent news articles**

  Check the Internet for recent news stories: doing a search on the name of the company can bring up all sorts of items from recent stock market flotations to charity events, all adding to your overall picture.

Other groundwork—the tools of the trade

Having the right items to hand will make sure that you don't waste time when you want to apply for a job, and will help to present yourself well. Although you do not need much material equipment to produce a good application, there are a few things which it is worth buying to help you present yourself in the best possible light to a recruitment manager.

> In redundancy situations, some companies will be able to help you out by giving you time on the company computer to prepare and print out a CV, or arrange access elsewhere. If you are in this situation, do ask what help the company can give you: no company likes making redundancies and will want to support staff to find other work quickly.

- **Computer and Internet access:** These are your two absolutely essential items. If you or your family don't have a computer, ask if you can share a friend's, and check out what your local library or job club can offer. Internet cafes are available in most towns and offer word-processing as well as Internet access, though this is a more expensive option. If you use someone else's computer, save your CV and covering letters onto a USB drive so that you are not dependent on your friend's computer. Check the print quality of CVs, applications, or other information you need to send by surface post. Most employers will want to photocopy your application to circulate to the recruitment team, so you will need a sharp, clear copy to give your application a good chance from the beginning.

- **Paper:** White or cream shades are the most useful shades of paper: you should certainly avoid papers with a strong colour. Again, this is because applications are usually photocopied, and deep colours will not photocopy well. Avoid using ruled and/or punched paper for your covering letter which does not look professional. 80gsm paper is fine, though you may choose to have a heavier weight for your covering letter. If you find it difficult to write freehand in straight lines, buy an A4 size blank pad as these generally come with a ready ruled sheet to place below each blank sheet: the lines show through the paper. Try to keep to A4 size paper as, again, this makes photocopying much easier and looks more professional.
- **Envelopes:** Buy strong A4 envelopes so that your application is not mangled in the post system and does not arrive on the recruitment manager's desk ripped or with dog-eared corners.
- **Stamps:** It can be useful to check how much your 'standard' application pack of covering letter, CV and envelope costs to send by first class post. Buy in a stock of stamps at the right price, so that you will be able to send out applications without delay.
- **Pen:** Although it is rare for employers to ask these days for a handwritten application, such requests do still crop up, especially for some upper end retail jobs. There are also some companies which will send you a paper application form to complete. For these, it is worth investing in a good pen. Choose a pen that has black ink: black ink photocopies much better than blue. If you prefer to use a fountain pen, discard the one that blots at unexpected moments, and also buy a stock of blotting paper so that application forms are not spoilt by wet ink.

Handwritten applications

How good is your handwriting? Be honest. There was a period when many large companies used graphologists–handwriting experts–to try and work out the character of applicants. The practice is rare in the UK now, but if your handwriting is messy or illegible, the recruitment manager will give up trying to decipher the form after a while. Remember that a recruitment manager probably takes 1–3 minutes to read an application: if yours takes longer to read than that it will almost automatically be consigned to the reject pile.

Practise writing in block capitals: this is a skill and takes time, but the reward is shown by interview invitations.

Summary of Main Points

1. Decide what you want to do by thinking about your work strengths and weaknesses; what areas interest you.
2. Get a second opinion from someone you trust: their view might surprise you.
3. Make a short-, medium-, and long-term plan based on what decisions you come to from (1).
4. Research and arrange any training you need to achieve your plan.
5. Review your plan regularly, but not constantly.
6. Put together the equipment you need to start job searching: computer and Internet access, paper, envelopes, stamps.
7. Search for jobs using the Internet, your local Jobcentre, free press, and your personal network of family, friends, and contacts.
8. When you find a job that suits your skills and interests, avoid the temptation to send off an application immediately: take your time to research the job and the company.
9. Keep a record of companies and agencies which are offering the type of roles or are working in the sector you are interested in.
10. In short: think, plan, research.

3 CVs

CONTENTS

38
The essential items
45
Adding quality
49
Referees and references
52
Formatting your CV
69
Summary of main points

The literal meaning of curriculum vitae is 'run of life'. A CV is a description of you and your career to date. It should give its reader an accurate picture of what you can do now—and what you are capable of in the future.

Putting together a good CV involves the **Research** and **Communicate** building blocks. This chapter explains what information should be included on your CV and how to present that information.

The first sections take you, step by step, through the various parts of a CV:

- Essential items: the information common to all CVs from office junior to managing director.
- Adding quality: the additional items you can include depending on your work experience. This section is broken down into groups of information: personal, qualifications, work skills, miscellaneous items, and how to describe multiple posts.
- References.

CVs for different types of sectors (such as the performing arts) and ideas on the format of your CV are given in the final section of the chapter.

The essential items

Start your CV preparation by gathering together the essential items of information that must be included on all CVs.

- *Full name:* if you have an unusual name consider making it clear whether you are a man or a woman, as potential employers like to know how to address you correctly in any correspondence. You can give this information by adding your title in brackets after your name e.g. Kashmira Green (Ms).

- *Contact details:* if you want to have any chance of being asked to come to an interview, make it obvious how a recruitment manager can get hold of you. You should put in your full postal address, email address, mobile telephone number, daytime and evening telephone numbers.

> **Quick Tip**
>
> If you have an answerphone or voicemail message on any of your phone numbers, make sure that the message gives the right impression to recruitment personnel phoning to invite you to an interview. A message that is amusing to family and friends may not gain you marks in the recruitment stakes. If you are using a phone you share with family or friends, tell them that you might receive a call about a job and ask them to help by taking any messages carefully. You can help them by making sure there is always a pen and paper near the phone. Again, this all adds up to making a good impression from the start.

- *Educational and professional qualifications:* you can list your qualifications either in the chronological order in which you took them or with the most recent or highest qualification first. Use the first option if the job for which you are applying gives no particular emphasis in the job description on qualifications; the second option if a qualification is required or if you consider that your qualification will give your application extra punch. For example, if you are applying for a job which mentions in passing that a foreign language would be desirable and you have a degree in that language start your list with it. You do not need to give details of grades (apart from degrees) unless you have taken the exams in the past two years. Avoid giving school qualifications such as swimming badges, unless these are relevant to the job, say as a fitness instructor.

> **Quick Tip**
>
> Explain briefly any qualifications not widely known and what level they equate to. This is especially important if you have qualifications gained outside the UK, or if the qualification has only recently been introduced in the UK. Employers do their best to keep up with the latest accreditations, but there is now such a wealth of different accreditations, a brief explanation is always appreciated.

- *Interests*: employers like to read a CV which shows a person who has a life beyond work. This is often called *hinterland* and enables you to present yourself as a fully rounded person. Your interests may demonstrate that you have a personal interest in your professional life, for example, if you want to work in an organization connected with animals, you might list 'pets' or 'natural history' under your interests. Interests can equally be something completely different from your working life, such as socializing with friends, hill walking or tango dancing. What you should remember is that you may be asked about your interests at interview, so claiming to be very interested in films when you have not been to the cinema for years is dangerous. If you take an active role in your hobbies, for example, doing voluntary work or holding memberships of associations, details of your involvement should be included. Achievements in your interests should also be noted such as wins at sports, fundraising, organizing a successful local community petition.

Making language work for you: the one-minute presentation

Surveys have shown that an experienced recruitment or personnel manager spends about 60 seconds *at most* skim reading a CV to see if it is worthwhile reading the CV fully and considering it seriously. You therefore have one minute to put your case for being the right person for the job to someone you have probably never met before.

Selecting the right words in an engaging style gives the reader an idea of:

- you as a person: the way you express yourself and the information you have chosen to include speaks volumes;
- your 'hard' skills: these are measurable skills such as academic qualifications and defined work tasks/experience (for example, reception duties or project management);
- your 'soft' skills: unquantifiable additional abilities in, for example, communicating with colleagues and customers; creativity and initiative; motivating a team.

The sum total of these three parts–the **Communicate** building block of the application process–enables the recruiter to gain a picture of all of your personality and skills.

Career history

The description of your career history can be the make or break point of your CV. You should list your current or most recent job first and work backwards to the first job you held.

The information you need to include is:

- your job title
- the company name and address
- the start and end dates of working for the company
- a list of your responsibilities and/or achievements
- why the job ended.

Of these, the list of your responsibilities and achievements is the most important. The golden rule is to target this list at the job you are applying for. You will probably therefore find it most effective to first prepare a 'master' CV which lists all the tasks and achievements for each post you have held and then produce a targeted CV in which you select the tasks and achievements which are appropriate. You can add the catch-all phrase 'other relevant duties as required' to your targeted list to show that you do have other tasks. Below is an example of this approach to devising a list, based on Hannah's last job:

Full list of responsibilities	Targeted list for applying for the post of supervisor in a customer service centre
managing a team of 10 staff	include
handling calls from customers	include
writing daily reports for senior managers	include
backing up the computer files on daily basis	not relevant to the post
taking minutes of meetings	not relevant to the post
training new staff	include
appraising staff	include
health and safety staff rep	not relevant to the post

Making language work for you: conveying your hard skills

'Hard' skills covers tasks such as computer literacy, specialized skills you need in your current job, and the 'nuts and bolts' types of skills of any job in any career: for example, scanning, filing, and photocopying in the office, preparing vegetables and meat in the restaurant trade, bricklaying and health and safety awareness in the construction trade. Think about different ways of describing a hard skill. For example, if your job currently requires you to deal with people you could describe this as:

- handling queries from members of the public;
- explaining the aims of the charity to people at all levels;
- managing customer service issues;
- resolving consumer complaints.

If you have a job description of your current post, try writing it out again using entirely different words and phrases. Pay particular attention to tasks or descriptions that are exclusive to your company or job. It is easy to use your company's established jargon, and you need to be alive to the fact that someone outside the company might either not understand it, or associate it with a different skill set.

If you have no job description or are not employed at the moment, write down the work skills you have and see if you can create an alternative description of them.

The next step is to convey the level of knowledge or experience you have for each hard skill. You can state how long you have been doing a certain task but it would make a CV boring if you put the exact time length next to each task or achievement. You therefore need to use words carefully to give an accurate picture of your ability to perform a task.

Thinking back to the example above, you might feel that after two years in your current job you are very good at dealing with people. You could therefore add a little more description:

- experienced and skilled in handling queries from members of the public;
- excellent ability to explain the aims of the charity to people at all levels;
- enjoy managing customer service issues;
- thrive on resolving consumer complaints.

Such descriptions are often where job applicants are tempted to over-exaggerate on a CV or application form. Stating that you are 'fully conversant with PowerPoint' when you have only used it twice is unwise, because you will be found out very quickly. However, vaguer descriptions such as those used in the examples above are accepted phrases in applications. They convey a sense of your ability, experience, and interest but remain indefinite enough not to pin you into making a false claim.

The other trap to steer clear of is using long or obscure words to describe a simple activity, or using lots of words to describe an activity or skill that just needs a one-word explanation.

To make your list even more relevant to the job, put the responsibilities in the order in which they most closely match the job description. The job Hannah has applied for stresses training and appraising as key responsibilities, after managing the team, so she would put these at the top of her list, rather than at the bottom.

Developing your career history

At the start of your career, or if you are applying for a non-managerial post, keep to listing your responsibilities in your career history; for a management, supervisory, or other type of senior post, you should give a brief overview of your responsibilities and then list your achievements. For example, here is Joe's career history:

> **Administrator**, Foyle & Camshot solicitors, High Street, Dudley, West Midlands (March–May 2013)
> (Work experience post: ended when returned to full-time education). Responsibilities included:
>
> - reception and switchboard; greeting clients and taking them to the relevant partner's office; dealing with general enquiries about the firm; keeping the reception area tidy and welcoming
> - checking general email box and forwarding emails to relevant partners' secretaries
> - opening, logging, and distributing post; collecting post in the evening and franking
> - photocopying and filing.

Kashmira, who wants to move into a management position, needs to take a different approach to relating her career history, as in the following example.

Sept 2009 to Present	Senior Translator, Andre Gide Translation Agency, 47 East Lane, Manchester M1

> Responsible for all translations required by Radio Manchester from English to French and vice versa; managing the French department in the absence of the Director.

Achievements

1. Negotiating the extension of the contract with Radio Manchester for 2 years and the inclusion of drama translations in the contract.
2. Training new recruits in the operational and IT procedures of the agency.

When you are listing achievements, start with new business you have brought in or mention retaining existing business for the organization and move on to any input you have had on the operation of the organization. Kashmira could expand on the example given above, for instance:

3. Deputizing for manager when on extended sick leave, including monitoring budgets with the Financial Director: interviewing and recruiting new staff with the Personnel Director.

The additional detail subtly adds to the picture Kashmira is drawing of her skills.

If you have had a **career break**, as Hannah has done, you should cover this in your CV with a one or two line explanation. For example:

2007–2012: career break while raising family.

Hannah could expand on this to show that she continued to work during her career break by adding:

2007–2012: career break while raising family. Assisted on voluntary basis at local play scheme, as administrator.

If you have had a string of jobs or a change of career so that earlier jobs are not relevant to the role you are currently seeking, you can condense these as follows:

2000–2007: various jobs in the construction industry.

If you feel that part of your responsibilities from a previous career phase are relevant to your application, you could add more detail to this condensed version, such as:

2000–2007: various jobs in the construction industry, including responsibility for Health & Safety issues.

Alternatively, you could highlight the key moment where you changed career tack and follow this with a short summary of your previous work:

2008: re-trained in software engineering, after various jobs in the construction industry between 1997 and 2007.

Fuller explanations of career breaks or changes should be covered (if relevant) in your covering letter. Your CV should just contain the basic facts.

Enhancing your skills

Career breaks and career changes happen for all sorts of reasons: having a family, caring for a relative, the state of the market economy are just some of these. What is important during these periods is to keep your skills up to date and to maintain the discipline of working. Keep an eye out for what your local community centre can offer, as they often offer free or subsidized crèche places, while carers' organizations may be able to help with respite care during training courses. Volunteering on a regular basis can help you keep up a regular work pattern, as well as providing chances to extend existing skills or learn new ones. Becoming involved in mentoring programmes, for young people in difficult circumstances or families in crisis, and befriending projects for older people provide good opportunities to support your community and at the same time develop your skills in social care, teamwork, teaching, communication…

Adding quality: specific information

What information you choose to add to your CV over and above the essential items is up to you. However, the rule remains the same: only include it if it is relevant to the post you are applying for. Think if this extra information will give the CV's reader an extra insight into your skills and character. If you have received a person specification with the information on a vacancy, is there a way you can demonstrate on your CV that you have the 'preferred' items it specifies, in addition to the essential items?

More about you

There are a few other items which you might include in special circumstances to add detail to your personal circumstances, but generally you do not need to include these.

- Your *marital status* may be relevant if you are applying for a job in an organization whose main concern is families, for example, a charity working with family housing issues. Otherwise marital status is no longer a required part of a CV. The same applies to including the number and ages of children: useful for explaining your suitability for a post working with children or teenagers, but otherwise just CV padding.

- *Website address:* if you are applying for an IT job which involves designing, maintaining, or writing for websites, you could include the address of your website, if you designed and wrote it, to act as a showcase for your skills. Outside this narrow field, it is rare for a recruitment manager to be interested in, or have the time to look at, your website.
- *Driving licence:* only include this if the post involves travelling, such as a sales rep or a post in logistics.

There was a fashion some years ago for beginning a CV with a *personal profile* which gave an overview of personality and skills. This is no longer recommended as you should be able to convey the same information in your covering letter.

More on qualifications

- *Education:* include where you went to school or college if (a) you are within two years of studying or (b) the company requests 'full educational details'. In both cases, include details of all educational establishments you attended since the age of 11. You should always include details of where you studied for a degree. You can do this by giving the university name in your qualifications, e.g. MA (Oxon), Ph.D. (Imperial, London).
- *Current studies:* if you are studying for a qualification other than a degree which is relevant to the post, include details of what you are studying and a current grade (if there is one). If you are studying for something which is not entirely relevant, include this under your interests.

Quick Tip

If your current course of study means you need to take time off from work, you must be honest about this requirement in your CV or covering letter.

If you are still studying and are applying for posts before your course finishes, make it clear in your CV or covering letter when you will be available for work. Unless you are applying to a company with a graduate or college leaver entry scheme, prepare to be disappointed if you are applying several months in advance of the end of your course: companies are rarely willing to wait more than six weeks for someone to start a job at junior level.

More on work skills

As well as academic qualifications, don't forget to include details about 'untested' skills, which you have learnt on the job.

- *IT literacy:* an astonishing number of candidates forget to include this on their CV. Check what the job specification requires you to have and list the software programs your experience matches in the same order, for example:

> Fully IT literate, including MS Office 2010, Sage, Internet, email packages. Working knowledge of Dreamweaver.

Quick Tip
List your work skills in the order which they are most likely to be of interest to the company you are applying to.

If the job description has highlighted the essential need to have, for example, Excel or PowerPoint, you could emphasize this in your description of your IT literacy:

> Fully IT literate, including MS Office 2010 (fully competent in Excel and PowerPoint), Sage, Internet, email packages. Working knowledge of Dreamweaver.

If you are applying for an IT job, avoid the temptation to clog up your CV by listing reams of programs in their different release versions. Stick to naming those which tie in with the job and group the others under a general term such as 'and various other web design packages'.

> ***Quick Tip***
> Working knowledge implies a lesser standard of expertise, but an adequate level of competence. If you do have IT qualifications (e.g. European Computer Driving Licence, City & Guilds, ITQ) do remember to include these, drawing attention to software mentioned in the job description.

- *Languages:* always put the level of your fluency in a foreign language. Accepted descriptions are: rusty (for those who took an exam more than five years ago); conversational (able to hold a simple conversation); fluent (able to speak, write, and read with reasonable confidence); bilingual (full language skills).
- *Training courses undertaken at work:* these are courses which have not led to a qualification, but have given you additional knowledge or kept you updated on progress in various fields such

as law or best practice in a given area. If you have attended many courses, save space on your CV by a brief explanatory paragraph such as:

Attended numerous courses and seminars on best practice in customer services and retail law.

Enhancing your skills

Organizations are always keen to have qualified first aiders on their staff so this qualification gives you an extra advantage. Don't forget that first aid certificates expire so do not include this qualification unless your training is up to date.

Miscellaneous items

- *Staff involvement:* such as elected trade union rep, student union rep, health & safety committee member. These roles give a recruitment manager an idea of how interested and involved you become with the company and therefore what you can additionally contribute.
- *Publications:* a list of publications is usually essential for an academic post and may be beneficial in other areas, such as journalism. Outside academic research posts, if your publications are more than a handful, highlight just those relevant to the post, for example:

Numerous journal articles published, including 'New Developments in Recruitment' (October 2012, *IPD Review*), and 'Internet Interviewing' (March 2013, *IPD Review*).

Handling part-time and multiple posts

If you have had a career which has included having a part-time job in addition to your full-time job, or if you have run several major jobs at the same time, you must make this clear on your CV so as not to leave the reader completely baffled.

For example, Richard once held a full-time post, but also had a freelance job. He could explain this on his CV by including the full-time job in his mainstream career history and adding a new sub-heading 'Other Positions

Held'. However, if Richard wanted to emphasize the skills from the secondary role because they fitted the requirements of a post he was applying to, he could include it in his career history as follows:

> 1985–1988 During this time, I was employed as Office Manager at Allaboutdesign Co. until offered the post above. I was also able to use my free time to act as freelance photographer for Midwest Community Project, travelling to various events and photographing them for the Project's travelling exhibition and publicity material. The Project ended (as planned) in 1988.

Note that Richard has also explained why both jobs ended: an essential factor.

Referees and references

> You will find it a very good practice always to verify your references, sir!
>
> Martin Joseph Routh

At some stage of the job application process, a potential employer will ask you to provide references. References may be taken up prior to interview, or a job offer may be conditional on references. Potential employers will expect you to give the name of your current or last employer and at least one other person, who may be a 'personal' referee. A personal referee may be a friend, or professional connection with whom you have worked—a colleague for example or someone from a different firm with whom you have had close associations.

The decision on which people to give as referees is important. Base your decision on:

- who is willing to give a reference—not everyone likes this task, so make sure you ask your referee first;
- who is easily contactable—employers will want to take up references quickly so a delay while someone is out of the country will not be useful. If you really want to include someone who is difficult to contact, ask if they will provide a written reference addressed 'to whom it may concern' which you can keep, photocopy, and send out as required;
- who can give a full picture of your work or personality—not just one particular aspect.

Larger companies may have a policy that only the personnel department may provide references: these are usually short, factual descriptions of your job title, start and end dates, and salary. The most that they will say about your performance is that it was 'satisfactory'. The reason for this is that employment law on references can be a minefield, with employees suing for harm caused by poor references and new employers suing for misrepresentation. If one of your referees will only give this type of reference, look for another referee who will be willing to give more details on your performance.

You can include the names and contact details of your referees on your CV or cover this item with the short phrase, 'details of referees on request'. If your CV is already long, include referees' details in your covering letter. It is helpful if you indicate on your application whether referees can be contacted prior to interview. The reason for this is you may not want your current employer to know you are looking for another job. Potential employers are sympathetic to this situation and will not disregard your instructions.

The standard layout for giving a reference is:

John Smith (previous employer)
Chief Executive
Helix Design
Jupiter House
47 Jupiter Street
Liverpool L1 7GG
Tel: 0151 1231234

Many employers like to talk personally to your referee, so including a phone number is essential. You could also include an email address, especially if you know your referee can be difficult to catch by phone. Your potential employer can then use an introductory email to fix a time for the phone conversation.

Some candidates send copies of written references with their application but unless you are specifically asked to do this, there is no need to do so.

There are a number of errors made by job seekers on giving references. The commonest are:

- giving out-of-date details, for example the name of a personnel manager who has left the company for which you worked. Before sending off referee details, check that the details are still correct. If you are using a personnel department to give a reference, ask for the name of the person who deals with requests for references.
- giving incorrect details, for example an old address or a telephone number which is one digit wrong. Again, take the time to check.
- giving the names of too many referees: if the company to which you are applying asks for two names, give two names not four, so that the recruitment manager knows which people you want to be contacted.
- not explaining your relationship with the referee: make it clear by adding 'current employer', 'past employer', 'personal referee' after the name of the person, for example.

Criminal Records Bureau checks: Disclosure and Barring Service

If the post for which you are applying involves working with what is technically known as a 'vulnerable group', which includes children, elderly people, and those with disabilities, the employer will require you to undergo a check with the Disclosure and Barring Service of the Criminal Records Bureau. Up until 2012, you could arrange for this check yourself, but changes in legislation now mean that only employers can request this from the Criminal Records Bureau. You can still request a check from Disclosure Scotland (which covers the whole of the UK) but it makes more sense to leave it to the employer.

You will be asked to provide your passport, and if you do not have a passport, other formal documents such as a birth certificate, driving licence, utility bill. The checks take between two and four weeks, after which you will be given a certificate. If you move on to another post, the new employer may decide to do a new check, depending on how old your current certificate is.

If you have criminal convictions, depending on their nature, these may be notified to your employer in the course of a check, even if they are spent convictions. If you are uncertain if a past conviction will debar you from a particular job, contact the Disclosure and Barring Service.

For more information go to: https://www.gov.uk/crb-criminal-records-bureau-check/overview

Note that it is against the law for an employer working with a vulnerable group not to check to ensure that employees are not on the Barred Lists, so do not be surprised if you are informed that this check is being carried out. However, the role must justify such a check, so do query a check if you think it is inappropriate.

Formatting your CV

Once you have gathered all the information you want to include on your CV, you will need to decide how to arrange it physically on the page. The rules to remember are:

- make your CV follow a **logical sequence** so that the reader does not have to work out the chronology of your career.
- use a **style** that is attractive to the eye and does not bury the essential details in a mass of different font styles and sizes.

The sequence

Your CV is a story so it needs to have a clear path to it which your reader uses to understand your story. The two basic sequences that are used to achieve this aim are:

STYLE A

- Personal details (name, contact details)
- Education (schools, colleges, university attended)
- Educational and professional qualifications (exams achieved)
- Current studies
- Extra and unqualified skills (languages, IT skills, training courses attended, staff involvement, first aid training)
- Career history, starting with your most recent job and working backwards to the first job you had

- Part-time posts, again starting with the most recent and working backwards
- Interests
- Referees

Style A is best suited for anyone starting a career or below management level. To find the right person for a 'starter' role, where most candidates will have a limited career history, employers will be interested in educational qualifications, extra and unqualified skills, and any career or volunteering history to assess candidates' potential and experience. These enable employers to identify candidates who have the potential to develop new skills up to management level. Aim to use the first part of your CV to show your qualifications, etc. (which demonstrate your aptitude for learning new skills) and devote the second half to your career history, followed by interests and referees.

As an example of a CV in Style A, here is Joe's CV:

PERSONAL DETAILS

Name:	**Joe Smith**
Address:	47 Brook Street, Southampton SO2 1NN
Telephone:	(home) 0231234567 (mobile) 07950 124657
Email:	joesmith479@btinternet.com

EDUCATION

2005–2010	Southampton Priory School
2010–2012	Southampton College

QUALIFICATIONS

2010	GCSEs: Maths (B), English Language (B), English Literature (C), Computer Studies (A), CDM (A), French (B), Spanish (C), Science (B)
2012	BTECH

continued ›

continued

ADDITIONAL SKILLS

IT	MS Office including Excel and Access; email; Internet; Photoshop
First aider	St John's Ambulance, 2012

WORK EXPERIENCE

March–May 2012

Administrator, Foyle & Camshot solicitors, High Street, Birmingham
(*Work experience post: ended when returned to full-time education*). Responsibilities included:

- opening, logging, and distributing post
- reception and switchboard
- sending faxes; distributing incoming faxes
- checking general email box and forwarding emails to relevant partners' secretaries
- photocopying and filing.

INTERESTS

Music (garage, blues); football (support Birmingham City), first aid—joined St John's Ambulance Brigade, summer 2012.

REFERENCES available on request

STYLE B

- Personal details
- Personal profile
- Career history
- Part-time posts
- Educational and professional qualifications
- Current studies
- Extra and unqualified skills
- Publications
- Interests
- Referees

Style B's sequence is appropriate for more experienced candidates or managerial CVs. Its sequence may not seem as logical as Style A, as the educational qualifications (usually gained earlier in time than the career history) are after the career history. However, this style is all about focusing and targeting your existing work skills (rather than potential skills) to the vacancy. The educational part of the candidate's life is further away in time and therefore less relevant as a guide to performance and potential. At this level, recruitment managers are more interested in the work experience and skills of a candidate.

RICHARD JOHN JONES *The Maples, Rhosneni, Herefordshire HR26 2ZZ* Tel (h) 01424 123456 (m) 07891 999000 email@ rjjones@madeup.com	
CAREER HISTORY	
2002–present	**Design and Production Manager**, Arco Publicity plc, London NW1. Arco specialize in branding for SMEs, covering all aspects from concept to implementation. *Role overview:* to manage the Design & Production Department, producing all company literature, promotional and presentational media including website design and management; to work with clients on timely and cost-effective design and production of all media they require. Main Achievements • steady growth of department from turnover of £1m to £3m • attracting new clients with 90% client retention for more than 5 years • building a cross-functional team with a high reputation for delivering on promises to both external and internal clients, after a period of stagnation in the department • efficient setting and management of budget of £750K • creating company intranet, training staff in its use, saving approximately £15K a year in internal paper communications • teaching departmental managers the fundamentals of design for use in pitches to clients

continued ›

Including the heading of each section makes it easy for the reader to spot the information they need and to understand your CV.

Richard's emphasis on commercial and monetary achievements may not be appropriate for a post in a charity: focusing instead on public awareness of the company, staff relations and teamwork could be more useful.

For managerial posts, a brief sentence introducing the employer, an overview of your role and a list of your achievements in the role shows the reader what tasks you have handled plus your skills and abilities.

continued

<table>
<tr><td>1997–2002</td><td>Assistant Manager, Design Department, England & Sons, Berkhamsted, Herts. A small company providing design and printing solutions to local clients. Left to further career.
Role overview: to manage the department's daily operation; manage small portfolio of clients; assist the Manager in budgetary control.
Main Achievements
• motivating and encouraging the team during a period of recession and restructuring
• rebuilding client relations after a period of poor standards</td></tr>
<tr><td>1992–1997</td><td>Designer, Pop Promotions, London WC2. A small company involved in promoting a variety of pop musicians. Left to further career.
Main responsibilities included the design of promotional literature for pop concerts; presenting designs to promoters; liaising with printers and web designers.</td></tr>
<tr><td>1988–1992</td><td>Freelance Designer working for a number of local businesses and individuals, designing company literature and stationery. Due to family circumstances, I decided I needed a permanent post offering more financial security.</td></tr>
<tr><td>1985–1988</td><td>Part-time Office Manager, Allboutdesign Ltd, London W2. A high street print shop. I combined this role with a freelance photography project. A first job after graduating, which taught me the basics of print and design, client relations in a commercial context. Left to pursue my freelance interests.</td></tr>
<tr><td colspan="2">EDUCATIONAL AND PROFESSIONAL QUALIFICATIONS</td></tr>
<tr><td colspan="2">1979: 9 O-levels including Maths, English Language and French
1981: A-levels in Maths, Further Maths and Design (all Grade B)
1984: Degree: BSc in Design, Keele University (2.ii)
2000: Chartered Institute of Designers, Post Graduate Diploma in New Media</td></tr>
<tr><td colspan="2">EXTRA SKILLS: advanced IT skills in many design packages (including FrontPage, Dreamweaver, Photoshop, Quark); all MS Office programs; website management; good conversational French (used extensively at Arco for a number of clients).</td></tr>
<tr><td colspan="2">INTERESTS: Countryside and the environment—member of the Ramblers, the National Trust, the Worldwide Fund for Nature, the Wildfowl & Wetlands Trust; blues music; family (married, two children).</td></tr>
</table>

continued ›

continued

REFEREES	
John Arco *(current employer)* Managing Director Arco Designs 76 Upper Street LondonNW1 1HH Tel: 020 7123 1234 Email: johna@arco.com	Philip Johns *(personal referee)* The Small House Haven Lane Leighton Buzzard Beds LU2 9KZ Tel: 01674 121212

Richard fell out with the manager at England & Sons so he has chosen to include his current employer and a good friend as referees.

CVs for different sectors

So far, this chapter has covered all-purpose CVs which can be used for the majority of jobs, and focused on the chief demands of the post. However, there are some sectors which expect a very different style of CV, or information which would not be included on a standard CV.

If you have had a multi-faceted career—for example working in an office role most of the time, but also working **freelance** in another field—you will need a different CV for each role. If Richard decided that he will look for another office-based design role, but also see if he can pick up his freelance career as a photographer, he will need a second CV, as follows:

RICHARD JOHN JONES
The Maples, Rhosneni, Herefordshire HR26 2ZZ
Tel (h) 01424 123456 (m) 07891 999000
email@ rjjones@madeup.com
website: www.richardseye.co.uk

Landscape and Wildlife Photographer

EXHIBITIONS	
2012	'Views of the Unknown', Jack Phillips Gallery, Hereford. Landscapes exhibition with three other local photographers. 'Richard Jones' eye is assured and produces new and interesting takes on the Herefordshire landscape.' (Herefordshire Country, June 2012). All photographs sold (to private buyers).
2010	Landscape Photography Competition, British Photographic Society, Jermyn Street Gallery, London: Runner-up in Countryside category. Photograph bought by Shropshire Town Council.

Although Richard mentions he is a wildlife photographer, there is nothing on this CV to underline his skills and experience in this field.

continued ›

continued

2000–2005	Annual Herefordshire & Shropshire Photography Exhibition, sponsored by HS Feeds Ltd, run by the Herefordshire & Shropshire Advertiser at the Shropshire Hills Gallery and Hereford Cathedral Gallery (Exhibitions ended when sponsorship ended). Photos exhibited were purchased by the Herefordshire & Shropshire Advertiser, Shropshire Town Council, and a number of private buyers.
1997	'London Landscapes: the amateur eye', Deauville Gallery, London SW1. An open entry exhibition for which the best 200 (out of 2,500) were selected.
1988	'Landscape and Community', Countryside Gallery, Gloucester. Culminating exhibition of a three-year freelance project working with the Cotswolds Foundation, examining traditional crafts and the future for the agricultural community in Gloucestershire. Photos included in the final report of the Foundation to national and local authorities.

COMMISSIONS

2011: Photographing country churches in Herefordshire for the Diocese of Hereford.

OTHER

Taking stock photos for use in my design career with a number of design companies; several sales of photos for stock use to small digital libraries.

TECHNICAL

Strong experience and skills in film and digital photography.

Richard would need to back up this CV with a portfolio of his work, using a hard copy display book for face-to-face presentations, or his own website with a gallery, or shared photo websites, or possibly even film presentations using YouTube, Vimeo or other short video sites. The address of the appropriate site should be included on the CV, as this is one of the rare cases when potential employers will want to see evidence of design and creativity.

Although a CV of this type should remain clear to read, the creative nature it is attempting to convey could be demonstrated in a more interesting typeface and the use of small images within it. However, bear in mind that if you are emailing CVs of this kind, you will need to keep an eye on the size of the document to ensure that your email recipient's mailbox can handle it. Look to create a file no bigger than 2MB.

If you are aiming for a career in the **performing arts**, your CV will need to concentrate on your performance work to date. Here is a typical example from an actress who is just setting out on her career:

Elizabeth Menabney

elizabeth_menabney@nomail.com
07777777777
Spotlight: XXXX-XXXX-XXXX
Height: 5'9"
Hair: Light/Mid Brown
Eyes: Blue

Training

Central School of Speech and Drama, BA (Hons) Acting (CDT)
3 Years, 2008–2011

Theatre

Title	Role	Director	Theatre
A Muse of Fire	Anne	Hannah Bannister	Riverside Studios
Hugo/Climate Week	Boss	Lu Kemp	Arcola
SOLD	Anna/Police	Catherine Alexander	Pleasance Edinburgh
Divine Words	Mari-Gaila	John Wright/ Toria Banks	Embassy Theatre
Europe	Sava	Dominic Rouse	Embassy Studio
King Lear	Lear	Catherine Alexander	Central (In Training)
There's No Place Like Home	Kristin Hetzel	Sinead Rushe	BAC
Love's Last Shift	Narcissa	Dominic Rouse	Central (In Training)
A Midsummer Night's Dream	Helena	Dominic Rouse	Central (In Training)
Three Sisters	Olga	Katya Kamotskaia	Central (In Training)

continued ›

continued

Film

Title	Role	Director
Wasser (short)	Sally	Leonardo Re
Bad Habits (short)	Woman	Nathaniel Tomlinson (Pacifist Films)

Skills

Accents: Native RP, Standard American, Standard Scottish, East European, Liverpudlian (Good Ear)
Music and Dance: Classical Ballet (RAD Grade 8), Jazz Dance, Tap Dance, Contemporary Dance, Pole Dance, Choreography, Clarinet, Soprano (can read music)
Sports: Swimming, Yoga, Cycling
Performance: Radio, Voice Over, Physical Theatre, Clown, Mask, Puppetry
Other Skills: Improvisation, Devising, Writing, Drawing, Painting

Careers in the performing arts often combine a number of strands—**performing, directing, creating** pieces. In this case, you need to present each strand clearly and logically, as in the following example:

Linda Marshall
125 The Street London W1 7HH
Phone: 0788 123456
email: anyemail@anymail.com

Artistic education

M.A. Performance Practices and Research at Central School of Speech and Drama
B.A. Contemporary Dance. The Place, London Contemporary Dance School

Choreographic experience

> Including a link to short videos of you performing, or examples of your creative work performed by others, is helpful and sensible in these circumstances

Own work—RoadDance Collective

- Statues—<URL>http://vimeo.com/xxxxx</URL> Premiered in London in January 2012
  Subsidized rehearsal space offered by Central School of Speech and Drama, The Place, and Jerwood Space.

continued ›

continued

Linda Marshall
Page 2

- Helena—http://vimeo.com/xxxxxx — Premiered in London in January 2010
  Performances in London (Robin Howard Dance Theatre, BAC, Space Makers) and in Sweden (Abundance Festival 10)
  '*An intriguing piece … haunting imagery and movement*' John Lukes in The Dance World (15 January 2010)

Work as assistant director

- Pale Horse. John Rochas — In current development

Commissions

- Peleas et Melisande. Vocal motion Murano Theatre/Jacek Scarso — Premiered in September 2009

Achievement and recognition

- Deutsche Bank Award for Contemporary Dance 2008. Received for the creation of HitchhikeDance Collective — September 2008

Installation and Game creations

- Small Child—<URL>http://vimeo.com/</URL>000 — Current development
  Supported by iMAL (Brussels) and Arts Council for England
- Spotted… <URL>http://vimeo.com/</URL>000 — Premiered in July 2012
  Commissioned for the Shepherd Festival, produced by Theatre One and The Bush Theatre (London)

Work as performer

- Pale Horse—John Rochas — Current project
- Walking By—Candida Shaw — Premiered in July 2011
- Stop Start—John Rochas — Premiered in September 2011
- Transport—Martin Martenson — Premiered in June 2010
- Laboratory work—Simon Alexander — R&D in September 2009
- Return—Hetty and Martin Martenson — Premiered in May 2009

Teaching experience

- Associate lecturer in Choreography and Performance—Blundell College — 2013
- Cover for choreography classes—Hanson Dance School — 2012
- Panel member for auditions—Hanson Company — 2012
- Choreographic workshops—John Rochas — 2012
- Movement classes for children aged 5-6—Fraser Ltd — 2010
- Voice and movement workshop for young people—Fraser Ltd — 2008

Languages

- French, Spanish, and English fluently spoken and written

Alternatively, you can create a different CV for each strand of your work in the arts. One young performer has experience in performing, teaching, and administrative work and has created a CV for each. Here is her CV for her **teaching work**:

Emily Adams

E-mail: **eadams@anymail.com**
Mobile: +44 (0) 7777 123456
Address: Flat 4, 25 High House, Liverpool L1 1AA

International career? Don't forget to put in your national phone code

Teaching Experience

Current **WellKnown Dance Company:** ***Dance Teacher, Youth Group***
Dance teacher for WellKnown Dance Company's youth group, teaching weekly creative contemporary classes to 14–17 year olds.

2012 **WellKnown Dance Company:** ***Assistant Dance Facilitator***
Assisting Wellknown Animateurs with participatory projects in primary schools.

2012 **Specified Dance**
Big Dance, Trafalgar Square: ***Dance Assistant***
Part of the team that delivered Big Dance, Trafalgar Square. Leading workshops, assisting specified dancers in rehearsals and working with participating dance groups.

2012 **Time Stands Still:** ***Production Intern***
Working with a theatre production company to assist with the administration and production of several small-scale theatre projects.

2009–2010 **Smalldance:** ***Dance Teacher***
Creating and delivering creative contemporary dance classes to children aged 4–12 years.

2010 **Specified Dance:** ***Assistant Teacher***
Assisting Creative Learning Department in creating new choreography for Wisdom In Age, performed as part of Sadler's Wells Festival 2010.

continued ›

continued

Other Employment Experience

General employment experience supports the sense to the reader of the CV that you are accustomed to a work environment and ethos

Current **WellKnown Dance Company:** ***Receptionist (temporary)***
Receptionist and office duties.

Sadler's Wells Theatre: ***Usher***
Customer service, sales and evacuation responsibilities.

The Place Theatre: ***Usher***
Customer service, front of house and bar duties.

2012 **WellKnown School of Ballet and Contemporary Dance:** ***Admin Assistant***
Assisting with office duties including database and file management and compiling correspondences. Also the updating and editing of the new school website.

2010 **John Lewis:** ***Sales Assistant***
General retail responsibilities, including sales, care of stock, and customer service.

2007 **Howard Hunt Group**
Working for a large printing company assisting the Marketing Director with planning a company open day and updating client database, as well as occasional work as receptionist.

Education

September 2007–July 2010 **WellKnown School of Ballet and Contemporary Dance**
BA (Hons) Degree: (II)i

September 2005–May 2007 **Localtown Grammar School**
International Baccalaureate (IB): 43 points (out of 45)

September 2000–June 2005 **Localtown Grammar School for Girls**
GCSEs: 10 A-A*s

References available on request

CV information for **academic roles** is very different from standard CVs, and makes such CVs unusually long. In this case, the academic institution needs full details of publications, research, conferences participated in, teaching subjects, and successes. This enables the institution to assess not only your competence and relevance to the post, but perhaps even more critically that your work complies with the Research Excellence Framework (REF). This is the mechanism which assesses the quality of higher education teaching and determines the level of statutory funding the institution receives. If you are applying for a senior academic post you will also be expected to give details of PhD students who are being taught or who have received their degree (as evidence of your guidance and teaching of them).

COLIN PARKER: CURRICULUM VITAE

Address	Flat 5, November House, Cardiff CF1 9HT
Telephone	0112 123123
email	cparker@academicemail.uk
Employer	University of the South
Present Post	Professor of English
Date Appointed	1-1-1992

Education

1990-1991 PhD: 'The Waterloo Poets: A Reassessment of Implied Metaphysics'
University of Warwick
(Completed 18-12-91, Accepted without referrals 4-6-92)

1988-1989 MA: Continental Philosophy
University of Warwick
My dissertation explored the feminist theories of Luce Irigaray

1985-1988 BA: Joint Honours in Philosophy and Literature
University of Warwick

Teaching Experience: Full Time

1992– University of the South

Undergraduate teaching:

- Eighteenth Century Literature and Culture Literary Theory—from Plato to Queer Theory and beyond
- Biography and Life Writing

Postgraduate teaching:

MA module in writing factual discourse

- 1 current: PhD student
- 2 PhDs passed the post

continued ›

continued

Other duties:

Curriculum development, administration, & c.

Publications available for REF 2014

This clearly shows the reader you understand the mechanism and have works which qualify

William Blake and the Logic of Contraries
Edwin Mellen Press (forthcoming, 2013)
ISBN: (Not yet assigned)
Monograph
This book gives a reading of all Blake's illuminated work along with Vala, or The Four Zoas, in a radical re-reading of use of the term 'contraries' and it should therefore on the palimpsest of the Vala ms. There is a tight ofcus on Blake's use of the term 'contraries' and it should therefore be a useful class text for advanced level students (I use the ms very successfully in my classes), as well as challenge to the current critical framework which, in my opinion, distorts Blake studies at present.

Other publications

Books

One Step Ahead In Essay Writing and Dissertations for Undergraudates
(Oxford: Oxford University Press, 2002)
ISBN: 0198605056
Monograph

Essays in Books

'Christopher Smart and the Architecture of the Mind'
Ritual, Routine, and Regime: Repetition in Early Modern British and European Cultures, ed. Lorna Clymer
(Toronto: Toronto University Press, 2007)
ISBN: 9780802090300

Journals articles

'Thomas Sheridan and the Second Smock-Alley Theatre Riot', New Hibernia Review/Iris Eireannach nua, Volume 4 No. 3 (Fall, 2000) pp. 65–77'
ISBN: 10923977
Publisher: University of St. Thomas, St. Paul, Minnesota.

Applying for grants is a key skill in a academic professions. Showing that you know how to make a bid—and have been successful—is essential.

Grant applications

I have been the recipient of a number of grants for research leave from the University of the South. I was also the recipeitn of a British Academy small research grant (£7,020) for research into the Blake manuscript held at Littletown Museum.

PhD supervision

I currently have one part-time PhD candidate under my supervision. Patricia Fraser is at the early stages of her research into an Anglo-Irish woman writer of the eighteenth century.

PhD successes inlude:

Mark Brady presented his thesis after eighteen months' work, and successfuly defended it on 17 June 2010 with Henry Evans (Emeritus Reader in Philosophy, Bridgeville University) as external examiner. He has also gained a full-time position in the Education Department at the University of the South.

External examining

I acted as external examiner for the Hightown University MA in Research Studies for two years.

continued ›

continued

Contributions to conferences

My main contribution to conferences has been setting up and running the British Society for English Studies Annual conference at Stoke College, Oxford for ten years. The conference is a major understanding, with 300 papers a year. The conference moved to Stoke College under my auspices and now brings the society between £6,000 and £10,000 a year.

Conference papers

American Society for Eighteenth-Century Studies, Vancouver, Canada, 16–19 March 2000, 'A Brief History of the Blind'.

Senior management posts will also require a different approach. The higher up the career ladder you climb, the more the emphasis your CV should place on achievements, with a corresponding lessening of the description of actual tasks. Even if you are not actively looking for a job, it can be useful to revisit your CV on a regular basis and add achievements as they happen, so you have an immediate starting point when you do decide to move on and up. You will probably find that concentrating on two or three posts which are most relevant to the role you want move on to works best, and reduce earlier roles to a simple one-line description. Here is an excerpt from a CV of an applicant for a role which will involve taking a long-established organization with a strong union presence amongst the workforce into a new era of business:

> 2002–2011: **Managing Director**, John Williams Ltd, Cardiff
> John Williams Ltd, founded in 1975, supplies and trades mineral commodities to heavy industry in South Wales and Ireland. Originally a family business, in the 1990s there was a buyout by management and long-serving workers. The company ran into difficulties in the early 2000s as the commodities market began to change. I was headhunted by the Board to drive forward the upgrade needed to overall strategy and working practices to enable the company to take advantage of these changes. Implementing the new structure and strategy demanded clear and logical thinking combined with sensitivity to the history of the company. It was an essential part of this that the Workers' Representatives on the Board were supportive and this was achieved through ensuring there were no compulsory redundancies and that modern apprenticeships in various disciplines across the company were implemented. Over the course of the nine years I spent with John Williams, turnover increased from £14.7m to £70.8m, with net profits of £25m p.a.

John Williams has now diversified its original offering and is involved in shipping, mineral exploration, and sustainable energy resources, leaving it in a strong position to weather fluctuations in demand and market forces in any of these areas.

On paper, this candidate is showing his ability to implement change without upsetting a workforce (which could be costly in financial and reputation terms), in tandem with better profits and a more stable place in the market.

The style

The style of your CV can be a good way for you to express your personality whilst still keeping to a clear layout, but it can also be a minefield. There is now such a huge array of fonts, effects, and template CVs to use from standard word processing packages or to download from the Internet, that you can end up with an eye-catching document—for all the wrong reasons. Potential employers want something that is legible and logical: not a bewildering array of fonts, colours, and effects which confuse the eye.

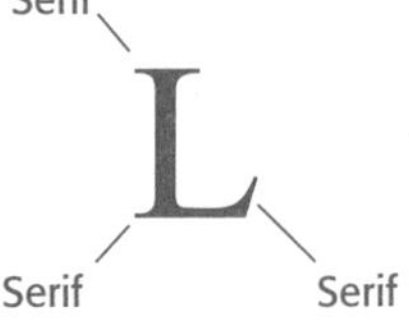

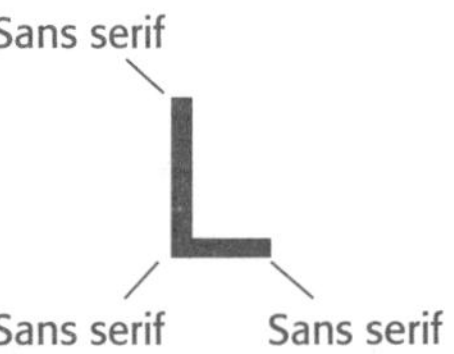

- *Fonts:* fonts fall into one of two basic types: serif and sans serif. Serif fonts, like Times New Roman, Bookman, and Garamond, have the extra lines at the edge of letters which many people find easier to read. Sans serif fonts, like Arial, Tahoma, and Franklin, have no edges to the letter. The look is sharper and cleaner. Avoid very fancy fonts, for example, those which imitate handwriting or have many curls. You should certainly not use a font which is rare and has to be downloaded specially as employers will be put off immediately from having to do extra work simply to read your CV. There is an ongoing debate on the merits of the popular Comic Sans font: it is recommended that you do not use it, as it implies an informal and jokey style which is not suitable for a serious document, such as a CV. Aim to use no more than two different fonts on your CV to avoid 'design confusion'. You could use one font for main headings and another for the text, or use one font for your personal details and the CV heading and the other for the rest of the CV. Use your selected fonts in a size that is easy to read, certainly no smaller than 10 point, and preferably 12 point.

- *Effects:* You can also use effects such as bold, underline, and italic in the headings or to emphasize a phase in your career, for example:

1997–1999 **Travel Consultant**, Maysbury Travel

If you decide to use different colours on your CV, bear in mind that when your CV is photocopied or printed (if you are applying online or via email) this is likely to be done in black and white, so your design intention will be lost. If you do use colour, aim to use only two colours in order, again, to avoid design confusion.

- *Layout:* stick to the basic principles of making your CV simple to follow and easy to read. Changing the layout every few lines is confusing for the reader.
- Using a *template* which is provided as part of a word processing package or which you can download from the Internet can be helpful to start with, especially if you are not an experienced IT user, but do check that it is relevant to the UK. American résumés are quite different from standard British CVs. Template CVs also have a tendency to try to cram information into one side, which employers can find difficult to read. It is also quite boring for a recruiter to be faced with 200 CVs all written in the same format: tweak your chosen layout to give it a more personal element.

What is the right length for a CV?

The standard advice for years has been that a CV should be two pages long. If you are just starting out on your career, it can be difficult to fill two pages: don't try. Recruitment managers would much rather have a one–page CV which tells them what they need to know without any extra padding.

If you have a longer career history, it can be a problem to fit everything into two pages. Again, don't try. Sacrificing essential experience and skills for the sake of perfect length is self-defeating. As long as you are sure you have focused your CV properly, it does not matter if it runs onto three pages but be certain you are not including details that are irrelevant or could be better covered in an accompanying letter. For example, your earliest jobs might only need the dates of employment, job title and employer name or your interests could be pared down to the bare bones.

Summary of Main Points

1. Remember that your CV will be skim read in 60 seconds by most employers, so it must tell your story clearly and quickly.
2. Create a master CV with all the essential information and lists of all your responsibilities.
3. Use this master CV to create a targeted CV, which arranges your responsibilities in the order in which they will appeal to the company to which you are applying.
4. List *all* the skills which are appropriate to the role: don't assume that employers will assume you have them.
5. Keep to the basic hard facts of skills and experience when you are starting out in your career; build your list of achievements as your career progresses.
6. Choose your referees carefully and ask them if they agree to be a referee if you are no longer working with them, or if they are personal referees.
7. Select a CV format that works for the information you want to present to your potential employer–and for the sector you are working in.
8. Keep the style simple and uncluttered. Avoid 'design' elements unless they are relevant to the post.
9. Your CV should be a page long when you are starting out; two pages for supervisory and management posts.
10. Choose your words carefully: make your CV convey your personality by your use of language.

4 Covering letters

CONTENTS

70
Introduction

71
Focusing

79
How to present yourself

85
Summary of main points

Introduction

A CV will tell a recruitment manager why you can **do** the job: a covering letter will explain why you **want** the job. A well written, well focused covering letter with a well presented and straightforward CV is a winning combination.

Covering letters come in all styles and lengths, from the simplest note saying 'please find enclosed my CV' to several pages of densely written, persuasive argument. These are the two extremes: a successful covering letter falls somewhere in between.

Using and developing the **Communicate** building block is probably even more important when writing your covering letter than it will be when you write your CV. Covering letters show:

- your competence in written English
- your ability to select facts and present them in a reasoned argument
- your understanding of the company and the job for which you are applying

This chapter concentrates on the selection of facts to include in a covering letter, as many covering letters are spoilt by rambling and irrelevant detail. Advice on structuring your letter and examples of covering letters are given. Hints on making language work for you are again given throughout the chapter, together with quick tips on other aspects of writing the letter, and employment generally.

Focusing: what to include and what to leave out

Your covering letter should not be a re-hash of your CV. Instead, you should use it to give depth to the bare bones of the facts of your CV.

Explain your current situation

If you are in work, say what your job is, who the company is and, unless it is a very well known company, explain what it does. For example, Kashmira could write:

> I am currently employed as Senior Translator at André Gide Translation Agency, Manchester's leading translation company. The firm translates radio, television and film and supplies interpreters for conferences and business meetings. It is renowned for the skill and dependability of its translators and its commitment to high standards of customer service. After five years with this company I feel I have progressed as far as possible in my present role and wish to move into a managerial position, building on my experience in negotiating and developing new and existing business, as well as managing staff.

You should spell out your career aims in your covering letter. In the above example, Kashmira has explained why she wants to move on from her present job (lack of career progression is a very valid reason for wanting to move on). She could now expand on why she is applying for the post, as follows:

> The post of Assistant Manager for Foreign Publications, with its emphasis on negotiating and representing the company externally and the department itself at internal meetings, is therefore very interesting, as these are the aspects I enjoy most in my current job.

This demonstrates that Kashmira has grasped the most important points of the job and why they attract her.

!

Quick Tip: explaining career breaks

If you are not in work at the moment, explain briefly why this is and, if your last post is relevant to the one you are now applying for, refer to it. Here is what Hannah writes:

> *Following a career break while my children were young, I wish to return to a full-time post using my experience from my last post as Call Centre Supervisor with Macromaster, a company providing out-sourced customer care for a number of High Street retail chains. The post of Customer Care Supervisor as described in your job description seems to be an ideal match with my skills and career aims.*

Making language work for you: who are you?

What words describe your personality? Try drawing up a list of a dozen words: six of you as a person and six of you as an employee. Consider how you can include this fundamental description of you in your application. You might use the actual words you have chosen or think of phrases in the context of the application which will portray this essential picture of your personality. Here are two examples to show this:

- If you want to demonstrate your sense of humour you might include 'and I make a great cup of coffee' when giving your statement for being suitable for the post. Make sure, however, that humorous statements are appropriate: the above sentence would not look right in an application for a senior management role in a traditional organization. In this case you would consider whether stating that you have a 'good sense of humour' would be more suitable.
- If you are interested in management theory and like to keep up to date with the latest developments in this field, you might look at a way of including some of the latest buzzwords in your application. The caution in this case is that you use the words in context without appearing to be 'trailing' your reader or showing off to them. You also need to be sure you understand and can talk about the jargon: expect to be quizzed on what it means at interview.

- The important point to remember when conveying personality is to target it appropriately. From your research of the job and the company, what sort of person do you think they are looking for? You need to tailor the language you use to fit both you and the organization.

Demonstrating your key skills and experience

You should show why your past and current work experience and skills match the post you are applying for. To do this, read the job description, pick out the skills/experience the company has listed as essential, and show any parallels with other posts you have held. For example, Kashmira has already identified negotiating as a core part of the job she wants and has begun to show that she has experience in this area. She could develop this, as follows:

> As an example of my negotiating skill, during the absence on sick leave of my manager, I conducted negotiations with Radio Manchester for the extension of our contract with them and, picking up on the fact that their in-house drama translator was retiring, arranged for this aspect to be included in the contract as well, bringing in an extra £1,000 per programme for the Agency.

Finding parallels will be especially important if you are changing careers as it will not be obvious at first sight why you are appropriate for the job. In the case of Richard, he could write:

> I feel that my experience and ability to organize a department will be of particular benefit in this post. For example, the job description states that the need to assemble and motivate a team will be vital. In my current post, I have built up an enthusiastic team who consistently meet their targets and often exceed them.

When you are starting out in your career and have little experience to draw on you will need a slightly different approach. You should concentrate on your willingness and ability to train. This means that Joe could write:

> I am interested in this post as it requires the basic skills I have together with the opportunity to develop new ones. I find I learn new skills quickly [*showing the company they will not lose time while you are training*] as, for example, when I worked at the solicitors and was shown how to use the switchboard.

Making language work for you: conveying your soft skills

'Soft' skills can be summarized as:

- your ability to bring creativity and initiative to a job (for example, do you prefer to be given comprehensive instructions, or an ultimate target and you work out how to get to it?);
- the way you manage and motivate people, both colleagues and customers (for example, can you communicate and delegate work to a team, can you build up beneficial customer relations?);
- work preferences (for example, your like, or dislike, of working in a team, having a structured job or preferring a job which is different every day);
- your ambitions and how far you have progressed in achieving them (for example, wanting to make it to the top management level or preferring to be a behind the scenes person who does the support work).

Conveying these soft skills can be tricky as they are difficult to quantify and prove. One approach is to set up a list of your soft skills and to look for examples of how you have used these constructively in present or past jobs. Using a solid example of the outcome of using a soft skill is more impressive on a job application than just a bald statement that you claim to have such a skill.

For example, Hannah has included in her list of soft skills that she is creative when it comes to problem solving. Her two back-up examples of using this skill are below.

- Managing a 'problem' employee: no one had previously sat down and actually talked through with her why she was always late for work, rude to colleagues, etc. I took her out for a drink and discovered that she had serious problems at home which meant she was always tired and therefore irritable. I recommended that she took a week's leave to sort out the problems and changed her shift hours. Within six months, she had been made supervisor of another team, and had retrieved the situation with two customers who were considering cancelling large orders.
- Managing 'problem' customers: whenever we dealt with a certain client, the order always went wrong. I checked the records and discovered that the order was always placed by one person, and always changed by another person for the company. I put in a new procedure for this client, whereby both people had to sign off an order before it was processed by us. Their business with us increased by 20 per cent and there were no further complaints.

Hannah now needs to check which example would be most likely to interest a potential employer and include the relevant one on her application. You can often take your cue about what soft skills a recruiter is looking for from the advert or job description for the post (*see* Chapter 2).

Job descriptions and adverts have a further use. Take the words the employer has used in these to describe skills and re-use them in your covering letter, CV, or application form. This shows you have grasped the employer's key words (such as 'comprehensive knowledge', 'enthusiastic self starter') and can apply them to your skills.

Highlighting additional skills and experience

Look again through the job description and company information to identify less important matches, such as IT skills, educational and professional qualifications, experience in similar roles.

Kashmira has spotted three other areas where there are parallels and writes:

> As required by your job description, I am a graduate in French and German, have first class IT skills including MS Office and Outlook, and am experienced in organizing the workload of my team.

Where you have less experience but can show a genuine *personal interest,* include this in your reasons for being right for the job. For example, Joe has written when applying for a job with a music company:

> I have good IT skills and, as my personal interests include a real enthusiasm for garage music, I have a good grasp of this area of the recording scene.

Joe could add something about the garage bands he likes to further show his knowledge, and it would be even better if one of his favourite groups is signed to the company to which he is applying, as this could be another reason for Joe to cite why he is applying:

> I have good IT skills and, as my personal interests include a real enthusiasm for garage music, I have a good grasp of this area of the recording scene. I have been a fan of Agent Network, and their recordings with you, for several years and have attended several of their gigs. An opportunity to work in a company working with Agent Network and groups in the same vein would be genuinely interesting and satisfying to me.

Potential employers like to see enthusiasm—especially from people at the start of their career—but bear in mind that a popular job with a music company is likely to attract many more candidates than other more run-of-the-mill roles. But someone's going to get that job, so always give it a try!

If you claim knowledge about a subject always try to give hard evidence of the extent of your knowledge, but don't bluff: you will get spotted very quickly at interview.

> **!**
>
> ***Quick Tip: missing matches***
>
> If you do not have a required skill or experience you can say 'although I do not have previous experience of [*whatever the skill or experience is*] I am keen to learn about this and feel this is not an obstacle to my ability to perform the job'. Add a reason if you can for it not being an obstacle–for example, knowledge of the rest of the job, basic common sense is all that is needed, indirect experience. You should back up this point by demonstrating your speed in learning quickly.
>
> You need to be realistic about missing skills: not having a good knowledge of an essential, particular IT program will not be accepted, for example, but a skill or experience which is specific to the job or industry to which you are applying is likely to be tolerated, *as long as* you can give some evidence of your willingness to learn, or your capacity for learning.

Answering any queries the application raises

Pay particular attention to questions that the advert or application description asks you to include in a covering letter, such as your current salary or when you are available for interview. If you fail to answer a basic question like this, however good the rest of your application is, it will end up in the reject pile because the one thing you will have given definite proof of is your lack of attention to detail.

When explaining your salary package, you do not need to go into great detail about side benefits such as pension arrangements. A simple explanation as given below will be enough:

> I am currently on £20,000 per annum, with pension and private medical care.

If your salary is very different (£5,000 more or £1,000 less) to that advertised for the post, it is sensible to explain why you expect to receive a larger or smaller amount. Looking for a larger salary is obviously a good reason to change jobs, but a very big jump from one salary to the next will need to be explained by either (*a*) the difference between one sector from another, such as salaries in a charity compared to a commercial company or (*b*) the financial circumstances of a commercial company have meant salaries have not kept pace with the market rate. If you have a pay award pending, you should put this in your description of your current salary. If you are looking at a job that is on a lower salary, you again need to explain this. For example, Richard could say:

> I am currently on a higher salary than that advertised for this post, but because I am changing career, I fully accept that the salary will be lower and the advertised rate is fine.

It would *not* be a good idea to add, 'I would be willing to accept this *initial* rate.' An assumption that additional salary will be forthcoming will not be popular with a potential employer.

You should end your covering letter with any personal circumstances which affect your ability to attend interview or when you can start the job. This includes:

- any assistance you might need if you have a disability: for example, help with stairs; a sign language interpreter at interview.

Quick Tip: disabilities and the law

The latest equality legislation aims to help people with disabilities to have fairer access to the job market. The great majority of employers are now able to consider people with disabilities on the same footing as everyone else, but if you have a disability you should mention this at application so there is no confusion on either side. The law requires employers to make 'reasonable adjustments' to support people with disabilities to work for them, but this does not mean the employer must invest an unreasonable amount of money to open up the workplace to a person with disabilities. Employers should, however, look at flexible and home working, at supported working and other innovative ways of working. If they do not, why would you want to work for someone so narrow minded?

- if applying for a part-time post where the hours are flexible to suit the postholder, which hours/days you are available
- your current notice period. If you are not currently in employment, state when you can start work

Quick Tip: notice periods

If you have a long notice period check if it can be reduced. Being able to cut the notice period can give you a very real edge. Ask colleagues what company policy is, but be careful who you ask if you do not want your employer to know you are job hunting.

- if you are living in a different part of the country (or another country completely) to where the job is located, explain why you are interested *and able* to move. Bear in mind that if there is no relocation package mentioned in the job details, you should not expect a company to offer financial assistance for moves.
- any holidays you might have booked: use your common sense and defer applying for jobs in the fortnight running up to a holiday unless you are ready to return at short notice and can give easy contact details.

Quick Tip: keeping the best

You should not use the same covering letter for every application as the focus will shift, but do keep a copy of all your letters and re-use paragraphs which are appropriate, to save yourself time.

Keep a log of covering letters which gained you an interview and keep developing these as you are evidently on the right track.

What not to include

You need to teach yourself the discipline not to ramble in your covering letter. Keep to the topics described above and avoid the following.

DON'T

- repeat word for word what is on your CV. Simply draw attention to your CV by saying, 'as stated on my CV, I have experience in…'
- go into lengthy detail of what you did to get your educational or professional qualifications unless it has a real relevance to the job. For example, do not describe how you researched an undergraduate or postgraduate thesis and the conclusions you reached, unless you are applying for a job which is all about your thesis.
- explain in minute detail what you do in your current or did in your last job.
- write tirades against your current or last employer. No matter how badly a job is going, recruitment managers will not be keen to take on someone who shows little loyalty to the company: such people are immediately marked as troublemakers and will end up in the reject pile.
- make conditions about your employment other than those needed if you have a disability. Starting an application by stating that you are unable to work Fridays or before 10 a.m. is a non-starter, unless this is an application for a part-time or flexible-time post.

Making language work for you—or not?

Some books on CV writing will suggest that the 'best' CVs use the language of the marketing department, for example, dynamic, proactive, motivated, challenging, ambitious. Although this approach may be appropriate for a PR job, for the majority of roles below senior management level, they can often be counter-productive. If you describe yourself as 'an ambitious and motivated individual with a real desire to succeed and progress quickly in this role' when you are an 18 year old applying for the post of an office junior, you are less likely to be selected for interview than the applicant who has said they are 'keen to make a start in an office career, building on my work experience at college'.

How to present yourself: the format of your letter

Your covering letter should be no more than one side of A4 at the start of your career, expanding to two sides as you progress. Like your CV, your covering letter needs to follow a logical sequence. The following format is an accepted standard:

- *what job you are applying for and any job reference*. Larger companies may have several vacancies and you need to make it clear for which you are applying. Recruitment managers are always keen to know how well an advert has performed and review if any changes need to be made to where they advertise to attract the right candidates. You are the ultimate beneficiary of this process of review as you will hear of more jobs, so take the time to give this information.
- *what you are doing at the moment and why you want to change this*: your current job and your career aims.
- *what makes you right for this job*: take the employer's job description point by point and show where the skills and experience you have match.
- if requested, *salary details, when you are available for interviews* or *to start work*.
- *special personal circumstances*: as described in the previous section, 'Answering any queries the application raises'.

Use a font and type size that is easy to read: using the same font and size as your CV makes good design sense.

You can choose to write in paragraphs or use bullet points to list your skills or experience, for example:

I feel my most relevant skills are:

- verbal and written communications
- self-organization and time management
- commitment to the company
- speed and competency in learning new skills.

Finally, do not forget to sign your letter.

Quick Tip: checking it over

When you have written your letter and if you have time, print it out and put it aside for an hour or two. You often see places where you can improve and clarify a letter if you return to it with a fresh mind, as well as spotting spelling mistakes and missing information.

!

Examples of covering letters

The following examples show four types of covering letter. First, a standard covering letter from Joe responding to a newspaper advert for an office junior at a sports events organization.

47 West Street Birmingham B14 1PM
20 November 2012

Dear Miss Forbes

Re: <u>Vacancy for Office Junior</u>

I saw your advertisement for the above post in the Swansea Gazette and am enclosing my CV in application.

I have recently completed my BTECH and am now keen to start my career in a company which, as you say in your advert, can offer comprehensive training and experience in all forms of office administration.

As required by the advert, I have good IT skills (gaining a Distinction in this module in my BTECH) and have previous work experience in a similar role at a solicitors' office. I especially enjoyed the switchboard work this involved, and am therefore pleased to see this task has prime importance in your job description. As a fan of many types of sport, from football to snooker, I have an immediate interest in the main aim of the company and would be fascinated to learn more on the background of how events are organized.

I am available for an immediate start.

Yours sincerely

JOE SMITH

It would have been more professional if Joe had also put Miss Forbes's name and address before the start of the letter.

Next, here is an example of a speculative application from Hannah, following up a lead given her by an ex-colleague.

Little Barn, Market Basing, Northumbria CA4

Mr E K Hammond
H R Department
Thomson & Legat plc
Unit 47 Business Park East
Carlisle CA2
20 August 2013

Dear Mr Hammond

Re: Vacancies in the Customer Services Department

Mrs Rachel Greening, Supervisor in the Customer Services Department, has informed me that Thomson & Legat are in the process of expanding this department and looking for new employees. I am therefore enclosing my CV and should be grateful if you would consider me for any suitable posts.

Following a career break while my children were young, I am now looking to return to full-time work, building on my past 10 years' experience in Customer Service. As my CV shows, I have particular skills in:

- achieving high standards of customer service, with a demonstrable commitment to going the extra mile to improve the reputation of the company
- learning products quickly. I have kept up my learning and self-organizational skills through studying for a degree while raising my family
- telephone-based customer service
- database use to accurately log customer contacts to provide a full picture of the customer and form the basis of useful reports
- supervising small teams.

> I understand that Thomson & Legat operate a flexitime system and this would be beneficial to my personal circumstances. This, and Thomson & Legat's renowned stance on customer service, adds significantly to the attraction of any career with the company. I am available for work after the 1 September 2013.
>
> Yours sincerely
>
> HANNAH MASTERTON

Hannah has not put in a desired salary: from her colleague she already knows these details and is happy with what the company can offer.

The next example is Kashmira, applying online for a management post.

> To: jjarvis@jarvisandjarvis.com
> Re: Translations Manager, Hansen & Koch
> Atch: KAtkinsCV.doc
>
> John Jarvis
> Jarvis & Jarvis Agency
> 25 East Cheap
> London EC2
>
> Dear Mr Jarvis
>
> Re: Translations Manager, Hansen & Koch
>
> In response to your advert in The Bookseller for the above post, I attach my CV in application.
>
> A first class honours graduate in French and German, I am currently employed as Assistant Manager at the Andre Gide Translation Agency. I have been very happy here for the past five years but am now keen to put my management skills to greater use in a more demanding translation environment. The role of Translations Manager, as described in your application pack, seems to be an ideal position.

When sending your CV online, call it more than 'CV' so that the recruiter can find it easily when they save it to their own drive.

In support of my application I would note the following points:

1. Extensive experience in client liaison, building up good relations and developing new business possibilities with existing and new clients.
2. Strong management skills in team building through leading the team at Andre Gide during a long sickness absence of the Departmental Manager. I have dealt with a variety of situations from low staff morale to a case of absenteeism.
3. Sound budgetary experience, both setting and monitoring.
4. Respected translator of French to and from English in a variety of disciplines, often working to tight deadlines.
5. Good verbal and written communications, regularly contributing at management meetings, and writing for client and staff intranets.
6. Excellent IT skills.
7. Awareness of Hansen & Koch through their reputation in the industry, and a real enthusiasm to work for the company. The flat management structure and the emphasis on self-development is very attractive.

Emphasize knowledge of the company and its reputation.

You state in your application pack that the successful candidate will be expected to take up their post in January 2014. I confirm that I would be able to meet this deadline, as I expect to move to London during the latter part of December.

I am seeking a salary in excess of £35,000, being currently on a salary of £30,000. Current additional benefits include private medical care and personal pension scheme.

Information requested by the agency: do not include unless it is.

I hope that the above is of interest to you and and look forward to hearing from you. If you decide I am not suitable for the post with Hansen & Koch, please feel free to keep my details on file for future vacancies.

Yours sincerely
KASHMIRA ATKINS
Flat 6, 25 Manchester Street, Manchester M4
katkins25@btinternet.com

Finally, here is an example of how not to write a covering letter.

> TO: the person in charge of recruitment
>
> Hi!
>
> My name is Mary Connors and I'm interested in any vacancies you've got. I'm attaching my CV so that you can see the skills and experence I have.
>
> I' really interested in working for your company as it has a good reputation for staff development and training. Also, I've always been keen to work in your industry.
>
> Hope to hear from you.
>
> MARY CONNORS

What's wrong:

- Failure to include a contact address
- Failure to find out the name of the right person
- Over informal style
- No mention of what job Mary's interested in
- Spelling mistakes
- Emphasis on what can be got out of the company

Summary of Main Points

1. Don't make your covering letter a straight rehash of your CV: use the letter to add detail to the bare facts of your CV.
2. Use language to convey your personality.
3. Showing a personal interest in the company, and evidence either of knowing them through your current work/interests, or because you have taken the time to do some extra research, will help your case.
4. Don't bluff about your level of knowledge whether it is of a particular field, or a skill, or an experience. If you really want to work for this company, and don't have the essential skills or experience they want, look for other jobs where you could gain these—remember your short-, medium- and long-term plan from Chapter 2.
5. If you are missing an essential skill or experience, look for other ways to demonstrate your ability to learn or that you have an associated skill. Be prepared to be pragmatic: if you don't have the skills, you really can't do this job now, but look for ways you can learn them.
6. Look at different ways of explaining and demonstrating your keys skills and experience to give an individuality to your letter...

7. ...but make sure your language is appropriate to the level of the role.
8. Ensure your covering letter answers any specific queries the advert or application pack asks.
9. Mention any personal circumstances which affect an interview or the way you will carry out the role.
10. Always put your letter aside for a while after writing it, and re-read it later to spot improvements you can make to the style and to identify any omissions or errors.

Job application forms

5

CONTENTS

87
Introduction

88
Key rules

89
Core question: why do you want the job?

94
Additional questions

97
Technical issues

98
Common errors

99
Summary of main points

Introduction

When you have written the perfect CV and the perfect covering letter, having to complete a job application form can seem a waste of time. Too many job applicants fall at the first hurdle by deciding their CV and covering letter are more useful and send these instead of the form. But recruitment managers have thought long and hard to design a job application form which will provide them with all the information to make an assessment of your ability to do the job.

Recruitment managers who expect many candidates for a post rely on application forms to enable them to compare candidates objectively. Candidates answer questions appropriate to the post, so it is easy for the recruitment manager to determine if a candidate has the essential skills and experience.

You will need to use your **Research, Target**, and **Communicate** blocks to complete an application form. This chapter looks at:

- key rules for filling in application forms
- the core question of any form: why you want the job. Your answer can win or lose you an interview
- other questions which you may not always encounter but need to know what they mean
- technical issues on form completion
- common errors

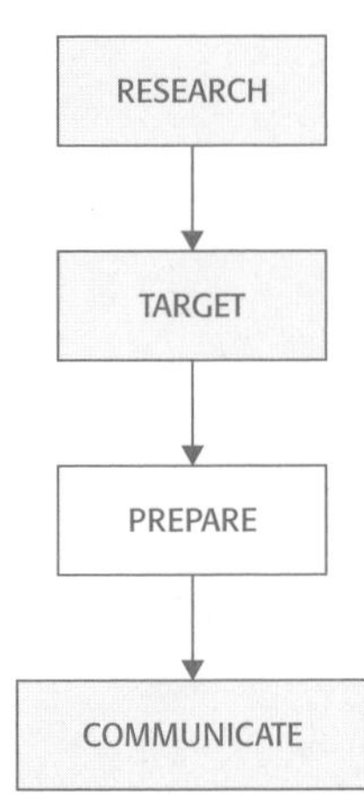

Enhancing your skills

Many people find it difficult to fill in forms for many different reasons. It is worth taking time to practise this skill (and it is a skill) because there are so many different areas in which the ability to fill in a form is essential: from a job application to a mortgage application, from registering with a GP to claiming welfare benefits.

Time is the important factor in completing an application form successfully. Set aside a quiet and unrushed time; take time to read the questions; take time to plan your answer; take time in actually entering your answers. The last is especially important if you are hand-writing your application form as it is easy for your brain to run ahead of your hand in writing. As a result, missing out words or making spelling mistakes are frequent application form errors. Try writing out your answers elsewhere first as a test run. Take a break from your 'rehearsal' answers then read them over again for errors or ways you can improve them, before you start to complete the actual form.

Form filling is a key skill in plenty of client-facing roles—retail banking, social work, medicine and policing are just a few—whether carried out manually or on-screen, so taking time to improve your skills in this field improves your ability to carry out these jobs.

Key rules

There are really only two key rules to filling in an application form successfully:

- read the question! The **Research** stage
- answer the question! The **Target** and **Communicate** stage

As obvious as these rules sound, a great many candidates fail to follow them.

Read the form the whole way through first and then give yourself a few minutes to think about what is being asked and how you can provide the facts required to present yourself in the best way. It is very enticing to rush into filling in a form straight away, but if you do that you invariably find that half way through answering a question you have either run out of space or have too much blank space left. Draft your answers first, to see if your answer is clear and relevant—and to check the space you need to make the answer you want to.

Be guided by the space element on a form. If the form gives four lines to enter all your education details, you can assume that qualifications are not especially important to the company. If the form gives limited space to describe your job responsibilities, pick those most relevant to the job you are applying for. Alternatively, group responsibilities together under a single heading (such as 'administrative duties' or 'financial administration') and explain in more detail in the space given for describing why you are suitable for the job. Conversely, if there is a lot of space given, recognize that this is the critical element of the application and the employer expects a full and detailed answer. In these circumstances, leaving more than three lines of space will tell against you as much as over-running the space allowance will.

> ***Quick Tip: educational qualifications***
>
> Where there is insufficient room on a form to list all your qualifications, select the ones most relevant to the post to give in detail and summarize the rest. Most employers will look favourably on candidates with English and Mathematics qualifications, so you could write 'Seven GCSEs including Maths, English Language, and English Literature.' Higher qualifications, from A-levels onwards, should always be given in full.

Core question: why do you want the job?

'Why do you want the job?' is an inevitable question on an application form though it may be given under other descriptions: reasons for this application, supporting statement, or suitability for this position are alternatives. This is the key question on any application form and the one you need to think about most carefully. Always take the time to write a proper response to this question: never just write, 'I've read the job description and I have all the skills.' This question is used by employers to assess not only how your experience and hard work skills make you suitable for the post, but also your ability to think through and write a clear answer. Therefore this question also shows your skills in problem solving and written English.

Read how the question is phrased to give you an idea of how you should tackle your answer. Some questions will be amplified by saying, 'Give reasons for your suitability for this position, drawing on your experience and skills.' Suppose that Hannah is applying for the post of call centre supervisor. First, she would need to look at the job description which came with the application form and spot the matches with her own career.

Job description	Hannah's matches
fully understand the product policy for which cover is provided by the team	know the products: this company was one of our big rivals in my last post
supervise team of 4 call centre operatives	supervised team of 6 in last job
monitor performance of operatives	did this in the last post
complete daily reports to management team	this was done electronically in my last post, but did give verbal monthly report

Hannah could now write in her supporting statement:

> Having read the job description, I consider I have the right skills for this post as I have sound experience of similar products to those sold by the company (as you can see from my career history, my last post was with Macromaster, which provided customer care for this range of cookers). I am used to supervising a small team, including their motivation, monitoring, and training. Macromaster had an electronic reporting system which I checked on a daily basis and discussed monthly with the Sales Management team.

More senior posts may require a different emphasis in your answer, as the reasons for your application may be expanded by asking:

- what you would bring to the company
- how you would approach the key tasks of the job
- how the job fits in with your career aims

In this case you need to read not only the job description but also the person specification and find out as much as you can about the organization you are applying to. If Richard has spotted a senior post with a charity he could write:

> I am very interested in this post due to its synergy with my experience, skills, career aims, and personal interests. As an experienced manager, used to creating, managing, and motivating teams, the challenge of setting up a new team is both exciting and well within my capabilities. My aim would be to form a team of people who would work well together, be able to meet deadlines and budgets by being aware of each other's work, and who adopt a hands-on approach. I understand that design and production has been a weak area in the charity, and I would aim to reverse this perception completely; building up the reputation of the department through promptness and reliability, so that it became a key and respected part of the organization.

When writing your supporting statement, again be guided by the space allowed on the form. For junior posts, keep to the space allowed, while in senior management posts, write no more than one extra side of A4, but only if the question states 'continue on separate sheet if necessary'. You should not take the invitation to continue on another sheet as a licence to write screeds: recruitment managers will be looking for a focused presentation.

Supporting statements are the one area on an application form where your personality can be reflected. By writing your statement carefully, you can let your commitment to standards, understanding of business issues, personal aims, or interests be shown in the language you use and the way you present yourself. Using humour (wisely) and enthusiasm can go a long way when you are starting out on your career and have less solid experience and skills to back up your application.

Quick Tip: reasons not to want the job

You should never include wanting a better salary or other benefits as a reason for applying for the job. The only benefit that is acceptable is flexitime or moving to part-time work if your personal circumstances require a change in your work pattern.

NI number shows Richard has the right to work in the UK

Insufficient room to list all qualifications so Richard has selected those most relevant to the post.

Note the question wants *responsibilities* not *achevements*, so Richard will have to include these in his reason for applying, if relevant.

POST APPLIED FOR:	*PRINT & DESIGN MANAGER*
NAME	*RICHARD JOHN JONES*
ADDRESS	*THE MAPLES, RHOSNESNI, HEREFOROSHIRE HR26 2ZZ*
TEL NUMBER	*(h) 01424 123456 (w) 01425 654321*
N I NUMBER	*PP 12 34 45 K*
EDUCATIONAL QUALIFICATIONS	
9 0-LEVELS, INCLUDING MATHS, ENGLISH LANGUAGE, FRENCH AND GERMAN *3 A-LEVELS: MATHS, FURTHER MATHS AND DESIGN (ALL AT GRADE B)* *DEGREE: B.Sc. DESIGN, KEELE UNIVERSITY, 2.II*	
PROFESSIONAL QUALIFICATIONS	
CHARTERED INSTITUTE OF DESIGNERS, POST GRADUATE DIPLOMA IN NEW MEDIA	
CAREER HISTORY	
CURRENT OR LAST POST: give details of job title, employer, dates employed, main responsibilities, reason for wishing to leave or leaving.	
DESIGN & PRODUCTION MANAGER, ARCO PUBLICITY PLC, LONDON NW1. 2002 TO 2013 *<u>MAIN RESPONSIBILITIES</u>: MANAGE DESIGN & PRODUCTION DEPARTMENT, PRODUCING COMPANY LITERATURE, PROMOTIONAL AND PRESENTATION MEDIA; WORK WITH CLIENTS ON TIMELY AND COST-EFFECTIVE DESIGN AND PRODUCTION OF LITERATURE, STATIONERY, NEWSLETTERS, WEB MEDIA. LEAVING DUE TO REDUNDANCY.*	

Continued over page

Example of a completed job application form

PREVIOUS EMPLOYMENT			
DATES	**JOB TITLE**	**COMPANY**	**MAIN RESPONSIBILITIES**
1997–2002	*ASST MANAGER*	*ENGLAND & SON*	*MANAGE DEPARTMENT'S DAILY OPERATION; MANAGE PORTFOLIO OF CLIENTS; ASSIST MANGER WITH BUDGETS*
1992–1997	*DESIGNER*	*POP PROMOS*	*LITERATURE DESIGN; LIAISING WITH PRINTERS*
1988–1992	*FREELANCE DESIGNER*	*SELF-EMPLOYED*	*DESIGNING FOR CLIENTS*
1985–1988	*OFFICE MANAGER*	*ALL ABOUT DESIGN CO*	*MANAGING DAILY OPERATIONS*
ADDITIONAL RELEVANT SKILLS *IT: DREAMWEAVER, FRONTPAGE, MS OFFICE (ALL), EMAIL.*			
REASON FOR APPLICATION (continue on separate sheet if necessary) *MY MAIN REASON FOR APPLYING FOR THIS POST IS MY PERSONAL INTEREST IN THE AIMS OF THE CHARITY. COMBINING THIS WITH MY EXPERIENCE AND SKILLS IN MANAGING A DESIGN DEPARTMENT GIVES ME A THOROUGH UNDERSTANDING OF ALL THE POINTS RAISED IN YOUR JOB DESCRIPTION. (CONTINUED ON SEAPARATE SHEET)*			
I confirm that the information in this application is correct to the best of my knowledge. I understand any attempt to falsify information will invalidate my application and/or any offer or employment.			
Signed: .... Date:			

An easy spelling mistake to makel

The smaller space allowed for older jobs shows the compnay is less interested in these. Include only the most relevant responsibility.

Write your name and the title of the job you are applying for on the separate sheet.

Quick Tip

You might find it useful to ask a family member or friend to read your draft answers or the completed form. A second opinion can spot errors either in putting your case clearly or spelling mistakes. In the above example, Richard's wife spotted the spelling mistake.

Additional questions

There are some questions you may not have encountered previously, such as:

- *Are you related to anyone in the organization?* Certain organizations need to be very clear on possible accusations of bias when hiring new staff. Housing associations, government departments, some charitable organizations, and financial establishments will want to know if you have any family connections with the firm. Such connections will not rule you out for the job, but must always be declared.

Quick Tip: friends and acquaintances

You would not need to declare that you have friends or acquaintances in the above circumstances. This could be very helpful for you to gain an inside track so do ask them for their views. However, do not call your friends at work and expect an in depth review of the company situation: ask them outside the work environment.

- *Do you have a conviction recorded against you?* If you have a criminal conviction which has not expired, you are obliged by law to declare this. The Rehabilitation of Offenders Act 1974 allows certain convictions to be counted as 'spent' after a given length of time. If you are in any doubt about whether your conviction is spent or expired, talk to your probation officer. Again, a criminal conviction will not necessarily mean the automatic refusal of your application: it will depend on the type of conviction and the nature of the job you are applying for. (***See also*** the section on Criminal Records Bureau checks in Chapter 3.)

- *How many days have you had off sick in the past twelve months?* Organizations advertising senior posts or roles which are crucial for the smooth running of the organization need to know that potential employees have a good track record on absence, to be confident that the company can be run efficiently. If you have had a poor year of absence due to special circumstances, such as going into hospital for an operation, add an explanatory note and give your usual number of days off sick. Organizations may also require you to complete a full health questionnaire, usually when medical benefits are included in the pay package. If the question is phrased as, 'How many days' absence have you had?' this does not include paid, booked holiday leave.
- *Proof of nationality:* employers are required by law to ensure that anyone working for them has the right to work in the UK. The simplest evidence of this is your National Insurance number, but you may also be asked to produce your passport, or, if you do not have one, a combination of other documents which the employer will specify. You will need to provide original documents, and the employer will copy these to keep on your personnel file.
- *Skills*: each organization will have its own approach to finding out from you what skills you have. This may take the form of asking you to tick boxes beside a list of IT software programs (often also asking you to describe your skill level) or giving you an open space to list your skills. If the form takes the latter option, select the skills which are relevant to the post, not every single skill you possess. The text shows an example of a completed skills list:

	No experience	**Occasional use**	**Daily use**	**Qualified**
MS Word			✓	
MS Excel			✓	
MS Access			✓	
MS PowerPoint			✓	

	No experience	Occasional use	Daily use	Qualified
Other database				✓
Sage	✓			
Email			✓	
Internet			✓	
Scanning		✓		
Letter writing			✓	
Minuting		✓		

- **Occasional use** or **knowledge of** means that you use this skill infrequently, or your skills are now rusty after a period of not needing to use the skill. Look for ways to brush up your ability.
- **Daily use** or **working knowledge** means that you use the skill on a regular basis and require little training to carry out any tasks using the skill.
- **Qualified** or **fluent** or **complete knowledge** means that you are thoroughly conversant with the skill and can use it with ease.

An alternative approach to a 'tick box' form may be for you to state your own level of knowledge against a list of skills. Use the terms above to demonstrate your understanding of each skill.

Do take the time to fill in **equal opportunities questionnaires** sent out with application forms: it is from these that a recruitment manager can identify whether its job advertising is reaching a wide range of possible candidates. If a company states that it is 'an equal opportunities employer' this means that it has a proactive attitude towards equal opportunities, and tries to ensure that its staff reflect the population in which it is located and the clients with whom it deals. Its offices will be fully accessible to anyone with a disability. Companies which are 'striving to be an equal opportunities employer' may have difficulty in reaching these aims, perhaps due to the layout of its office accommodation or its failure to get applications from people from ethnic minority backgrounds.

Quick Tip: keeping a record

It is very useful to take a photocopy of your completed application form. There are two reasons for this suggestion:

- if you are invited to an interview, re-read your application form and check what you wrote as part of your pre-interview preparation. Without a copy, you can end up at interview trying to remember what you wrote and wondering if what you are saying ties in with it.
- if you write a particularly good supporting statement use this as the basis of supporting statements for other application forms. No supporting statement will be quite the same for different applications, if you stick to the **TARGET** rule, but you can re-use phrases and sentences to save time and energy.

Technical issues

Use the following guidelines to help your application.

- Always write in black ink. Application forms are usually photocopied and black photocopies best.
- You will generally be asked to write in block capitals on a form: take the time to practise this form of writing until it is clearly legible. If you have real difficulty with your handwriting, one solution is to complete the form in pencil (lightly) and then overwrite the letters in ink, rubbing out the pencil afterwards. Even block capitals handwriting says a lot about you to a recruitment manager: illegible handwriting will take you straight to the reject pile; neat and clear handwriting will give you an immediate advantage.
- If you make a mistake on the form, cross it out neatly or use a proprietary correction fluid. If you make a lot of mistakes, it is worth calling the company to ask for another form and start again from scratch. Any more than six mistakes implies carelessness. If you are prone to making mistakes opt for completing the form in pencil first, then inking it in.
- If you need to use extra sheets of paper to complete your application, always write your name and the post for which you are applying at the top of each sheet. Do not staple the sheets

to the application form: use a paperclip instead as the staple will only be removed for photocopying.

- You can word process your answers by printing them out on plain paper, then cutting and pasting on to the right place on the application form. However, you need to do this very neatly, otherwise the precision of the typing can be very quickly offset by a first impression of messiness.

Common errors

Application forms are deceptive: they can look easy to complete and therefore encourage you to be careless. Bear the following in mind and avoid the most common errors.

- *failing to complete the form:* easily done if you complete half the form and then put it aside for a while. Read the form through again before putting it in an envelope.
- *not checking the spelling*: spelling mistakes—especially very simple ones—occur more frequently if you write in block capitals. Again, take the time to read through the form before sending it off.

Making language work for you: write it right

How good is your spelling? Check an application form word for word with a dictionary and see how many errors you have made. Keep a list of the words you have misspelt for quick reference for future applications. Expand your list as you complete more forms.

If you are word processing your application, don't rely on the spell checker program as it will miss words correctly spelt but used in the wrong context, for example:

where	were
there	their
would have	would of
wood	would

- *do not use texting language:* write in full English.
- *putting the wrong company name or job title in:* this tends to happen if you word process answers and stick them on to your application form.
- *being too literal or too honest in your replies:* Here are a selection of answers demonstrating this point. They were guaranteed to make the recruitment managers involved laugh, but they did not get the applicant an interview.

Last employer: Julie, the floor manager
Reason for leaving: I was dismissed
Reason for leaving: Caught my hand in the toaster
Reason for applying: My lecturer gave me the form

Summary of Main Points

1. Remember the two key rules: read the question, answer the question.
2. Read the whole form through and draft your answers before filling in the actual form.
3. Be guided by the space given to a particular question: the larger the space the more important the answer to the question is for the employer.
4. You should spend most time and energy answering the 'why you want the job' question, matching your skills, experience, and personal interest in the role to the job description.
5. Concentrate on the work aspects of the role for wanting the post, not a higher salary or other benefits.
6. If your reasons for wanting the job flow onto an additional sheet, always put your name and the post for which you are applying at the top of the sheet.
7. Double-check your spelling.
8. Check that you have completed the whole form.
9. Ask a friend or family member to read your completed application through before sending it out.
10. Keep a copy of your application for referral if you are offered an interview, and for future applications if you have written a particularly good answer to a question.

6 Online applications

CONTENTS

100
Introduction

100
Application forms online

105
Online or email CVs and covering letters

106
The pitfalls

109
Summary of main points

Introduction

Online applications are, naturally, the norm for registering with online recruitment agencies, and many of the traditional agencies and larger employers also use this method. Candidates and recruitment managers alike favour the speed at which applications can be made and received, the reduction in paper and storage required, and the decrease in postage costs.

An online application system also enables employers to test applicants' vocational skills and to measure their potential in a particular sector or role.

This chapter looks at what you are likely to encounter when making an online application and how to make full use of this recruitment method. It also highlights and shows you how to avoid some of the common pitfalls.

Smaller companies will usually ask you to simply email your CV with a covering letter. This chapter also looks at such applications and again gives advice on steering clear of frequent errors.

Application forms online

The larger commercial companies, recruitment agencies, and HR consultants generally use a combined online application system. This means that you will be asked to complete an on-screen form, and to submit your CV.

Recruitment companies use their online application systems to build up a profile of your core skills and experiences. This profile can then be matched by computer against any suitable vacancies. The form will consist of a number of screens:

- **basic information:** name, contact details, the type of post you are looking for in which sector, salary
- **skills:** your IT, language and skills specific to your sector or job type
- **key words:** this is one of the most important fields to take time to think about when you are registering with an agency, as these are the words the agency will search on to match you against opportunities it has. Group your skills under headings such as administration, finance, IT. If you find the agency is consistently emailing you details of the wrong type of job, delete your profile and start again
- **job title:** another way for the agency to search for the right person from its database. Be careful if you use a job title that has different meanings in different sectors, and also avoid being too prescriptive as this can inadvertently shut you out of potential vacancies
- **work history:** this is usually cut down to the last two posts
- **tests:** ***see*** the next section, 'Online tests', for more details on these
- **covering letter:** don't rush into filling this section in. You will get better results if you draft a couple of different paragraphs before you start looking at websites. Focus your paragraphs according to the type of job the agency offers. Here are two paragraphs Kashmira has written, the first for use on management recruitment sites and the second for use on translation vacancy sites, as follows:

1. Following a solid grounding as a deputy manager, I am keen to move into a more responsible managerial role in a business which will make use of my languages, ability to lead and develop junior staff and to build up relations with clients.
2. As an experienced translator in French with Manchester's leading translation agency, I am now looking for opportunities as a translator with a commercial company.

Both paragraphs accurately describe Kashmira's skills and aims, but their focus is entirely different and will bring different results.

Quick Tip

Some agencies will specify that you can only use a certain number of words to write your profile so keep a record of the word count for each version of your profile. You could also see how many words you can cut or add to the same profile to give the same effect but with fewer or more words.

Check also whether the limit is on words or characters. If the limit is on characters, this reduces the number of words you can use, as each space and punctuation mark must be added into the calculation.

The points to remember when completing an online application are:

- *read the instructions:* the opening screen should tell you what information must be completed; whether you can save part of your application and return to it later if you need to stop mid-way through; the additional documents, such as a CV, which you will be expected to attach
- allow yourself sufficient *time* to complete the form with as much care as you would a standard postal application. Websites will sometimes give an indication of how long the screens will take to complete, but always allow at least an hour to do yourself justice.
- *check and revise* your profile on a regular basis. Explore the vacancies on the website. If you have not been notified of jobs you are interested in, make a list of the key words used in describing these jobs and include them in your profile. Buzz words change quite quickly and you need to keep your profile up to date.

One problem with online application forms is that their 'one size fits all' may not exactly match your personal career circumstances. If you have taken a sideways move recently, such as filling in time between jobs by temping while looking for something more suitable, this can give your career history an incoherent look. If so, fill in the last two most relevant positions: appropriate skills and experience are of more use to the recruitment consultant than exact career chronology. Your accompanying CV should remain in date order, but explain any unexpected career moves and give prominence to the posts giving suitable work experience.

Online tests

An online application system may include vocational or personality tests. These are used by recruitment agencies to assess your level of competence, and by employers to identify the candidates who have the relevant skills for the job.

Vocational tests could be in:

- general-use IT programs such as MS Word, Excel, Outlook and PowerPoint. Recruitment agencies will usually tell you your score in these. Keep the record of these scores, as you might be able to include them in applications for other posts. You could also see how your skills are progressing, if you take a similar or the same test for another agency later on

> ***Quick Tip: revising***
>
> Just as you revised for exams, if you know there is a test being included in the recruitment process (whether online or in a face-to-face setting, revise for the test. IT skills, especially the ability to type accurately, can be lost if not used regularly, so do take the time to brush up regularly, and particularly when you have a test coming up. If you do not have ready access to a PC, ask friends, use an Internet café, your local library or community centre.

- IT software specific to your career sector such as Sage, SAP, or other accountancy software; consumer databases; fundraising software such as Raiser's Edge. If you are just starting out in your career, check what the industry standard software is and consider investing in a training course if you realize that every job you look at asks for competency in it
- a test designed to check your competency in a number of different disciplines, for example reading a document containing data, which you are then asked to input to a spreadsheet and, from this, produce a report. This will check your ability to read and interpret data, to create a spreadsheet and use it to make a report and, importantly, your ability to understand and adhere to the instructions of the test.

The online application will generally tell you how long each test will take and may indeed require you to complete it within a given time, after which the test will automatically close. Make sure you have sufficient time generally to do the test as it would be very frustrating if you have booked a one-hour slot on a PC at a library or community centre and have to stop midway through. Try as far as possible to be in a quiet environment and if you are using a PC at a shared location, such as a library, explain to the staff what you want to do: they may be able to fix you a session in a private room or suggest the quietest times of the day. If you are doing your test at home, make sure your Internet connection is reliable. It is unlikely that anything other than a broadband connection will have sufficient processing power for the amount of data and the time allowed.

Online psychometric tests are designed to check what roles would suit your personality and career aims best. The tests can consist of:

- descriptions of work and personal scenarios where you are asked to select from a given range of actions you could take to resolve problems in the scenarios. The more complex tests may use your answers to the initial scenario to take you forward to a further development in the scenario when you again have a choice to make from a range of answers, and so on.
- a series of statements. You will be asked to select the statement which you most closely agree with, for example:

  - I like to work in a team.
  - I like to work by myself.

  The more complicated tests will gradually narrow the difference between the statements and make obvious choices of the 'right' answer more difficult, for example:

  - I value customer service.
  - I value customer retention.

- reasoning or IQ tests, designed to see in what way you work. These are mainly aimed at management-level jobs and look for your potential to work logically or instinctively, or to use a mixture of both.

There is no right or wrong answer in any psychometric test which has been properly designed. They are aimed at finding out your strengths and weaknesses for a role with that company alone. The general rule on these tests is to do them quickly, without giving yourself too much time to think: test results are most accurate if you use your instinct in answering rather than manipulating your answers to what you *think* the company wants to hear.

> **Quick Tip**
>
> If you find yourself trying to pick the 'right' answer the chances are you are not applying for the 'right' job: this is a warning sign that if you do get the job, you will have little personal satisfaction in the role. This can sometimes be an awakening when you realize that what you think is your chosen role or career sector turns out to be incompatible with your personality. Look on this positively: you could have ended up being miserable for the next 20 or 30 years! The tests will often give you a hint of where your personality traits could be appreciated and where you will find genuine job satisfaction.

Online or email CVs and covering letters

The basic rule for submitting your CV online is the same as for postal applications: focus your CV and letter so that you are applying for the job advertised, not for a universal job that never existed. Here are some extra tips.

- Most recruitment agencies have tips on writing CVs as part of their website: take time to read these pages and then incorporate the tips in your own CV so that you are sure you are submitting exactly what the agency wants to see.
- If you are sending a speculative application, don't send it to the email address of the manager of an individual department: look on the website for the careers/jobs email address or that of the HR manager. Doing this will prevent your application getting lost in the usual business emails of a manager, or sitting in a redundant mailbox. If you are not sure what the correct email address is, ring and ask, but be prepared to be told that the organization is not accepting speculative applications.

- Your covering letter does not need to be sent as a separate document if you are applying by email. The email itself can serve as your covering letter.

Making language work for you

Write the email as you would write a paper-based covering letter, starting with 'Dear (name of recipient)' and finishing 'Yours sincerely'.

Always use the surname of the person in the salutation of your covering letter (e.g. 'Dear Miss Leigh', 'Dear Mr Wedderburn'). Don't use the first name of the person in your salutation of your covering letter (e.g. 'Dear Judith', 'Dear Harry'). When addressing a woman whose marital status you don't know, use the catch-all Ms.

- When an advert for a post says to send just a CV, your accompanying email should still make it clear which post you are applying for. For example:

  Dear Mrs Varley
  Please find attached my CV in application for the post of Fundraising Administrator.

  Yours sincerely
  JOE SMITH

  Include the title of the post in the subject line of the email, so that the recipient can tell at a glance why you are writing to them.

The pitfalls

The old adage 'more haste, less speed' rings particularly true for electronic applications.

The main problem with sending an electronic application is the temptation to send it immediately, without checking the facts of the job or what the company actually does. Recruitment managers can virtually rely on dismissing the first half-dozen CVs they receive by email, because they have been sent by candidates using a 'scatter gun' approach to applications, in the hope that one will stick somewhere. The fact that you got your application in an hour after the advert appeared gives it no weight against the candidate who applied a day or two later with a properly focused application.

Common pitfalls of electronic applications fall into two categories: **technical** and **style**.

Technical

- *Sending large attachments as part of your application:* In a survey carried out by Reed.co.uk, 48 per cent of recruitment managers said 'that they would automatically bin a CV with fancy video clips or any large, cumbersome attachment'. Company email systems are usually set up not to receive emails with over-large attachments. Keep attachments to less than 2MB.
- *Asking the recruitment manager to look at your website* for all the appropriate information is not a good idea. Why should the recruitment manager bother when there will be other candidates who will have sent all the relevant information with the email?
- *Sending an application which contains a virus* is an immediate way of ensuring your application will be rejected. If you have your own PC, invest in decent anti-virus software and use it to run scheduled checks, according to the manufacturer's instructions. Check all attachments for viruses before you send them. If you are using a PC in a library, ask the library how they check for viruses and ask if you can check the documents you want to attach.

Quick Tip

Use your website as a supporting tool in your application, not the main resource. For example, you could include your website address on your CV so that an interested recruitment manager can look it up, but accept that they are fairly unlikely to do so.

- If you are *using someone else's email address* to send your application, it is worth explaining this in your email. For example:

  Please note that I am using a friend's email address to send this application to you. Replies to this email address will be passed on to me within a couple of hours.

  Don't forget to agree with your friend that they will pass on emails in a given time!

- *Using a sophisticated design format* within your email, such as text boxes, tables, and bullet points: unless the recruitment manager uses the same software as you, this formatting can get lost in transmission, leaving the recruitment manager with pages of gobbledegook. If you want to make points in your email, stick to typing 1, 2, 3, etc. rather than using the program's function to enter these numbers.

Quick Tip

Be wary of using anything other than a standard style of email format. If you use, for example, a coloured or photograph background or an electronic signature, the recipient's virus checker may block it, or not download it correctly. Your intention to create a good and innovative first impression may therefore be lost in the recipient's irritation at not being able to read your email.

STYLE

- *Using an inappropriate format* for your CV, for example MS PowerPoint or MS Publisher. PowerPoint was designed for personal presentations at face-to-face meetings and, harking back to a technical point, PowerPoint documents take too long to download. Publisher is not a program used by everyone, so the recruitment manager may not be able to open the document and that will guarantee a rejection.
- If you are applying for a design post, you might be asked to supply examples of your work in a variety of formats, but this is the only time that *sending personal promotional documents* (other than your CV) with an application is appropriate.

- *Taking a jokey, over-informal approach* to the application, such as writing 'Hi!' in the message field of the application. However laid back the company, they will still expect you to take your application seriously, otherwise why should they take you seriously?Make sure your *email address is appropriate.* While zogfromplanettharg@btinternet.com might have amused your friends and family, it will say heaps about you—and not necessarily the right things—to a recruitment manager. Most Internet companies will allow you a couple of addresses: keep the joke one for personal emails and have one with your name, or an abbreviation of your name, for business purposes.

Summary of Main Points

1. Remember you should treat an online application in the same way as a paper application, using the same building blocks of research, target, and communicate.
2. Read through on-screen applications first before starting to complete them; draft your supporting statement as for a paper application.
3. When registering on recruitment sites, be careful in selecting what key words you decide to attach to your profile and the job titles you are interested in, to ensure that you receive jobs that best match your career interests and skills.
4. Follow the instructions and tips on recruitment agency or career websites to ensure your CV and profile contain the information the company wants and are in their preferred format.
5. Regularly review any profile and CVs you register online.
6. If an online application involves a test, check what skills it will examine and revise for it first.
7. Email covering letters need to be as formal as a paper application.
8. Use a standard format and font for your emails to ensure that they are easy for the recipient to read.
9. Keep email attachments short and simple.
10. The golden rule: take your time. It is too easy to be tempted to send your application before you've focused and checked it.

7 Speculative applications

CONTENTS

110
Introduction

111
Which job?

112
Which company?

114
Target and communicate your application

119
Summary of main points

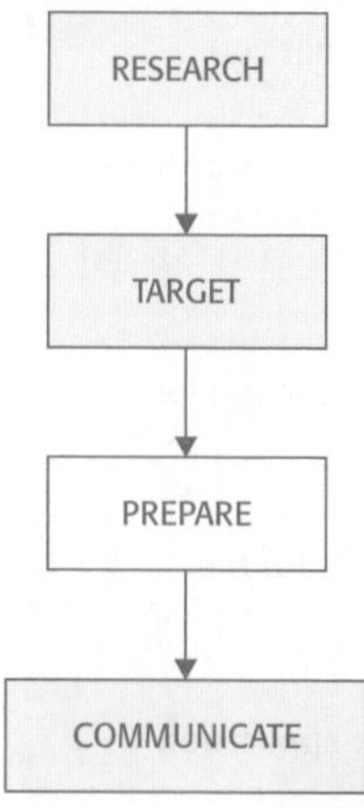

Introduction

Applying for a job you know exists is the easier end of the job hunt. What happens if you can't find the job you want in the adverts but know roughly what you want to do and who you want to work for?

Speculative applications are a test for your communication skills. You need to persuade a company which didn't know it needed you that you are indispensable. Speculative applications combine three of the building blocks of the job hunt: you will need to **Research** your own experience, skills, and interests and the market in which they will be valuable; you will need to **Target** your application precisely, and finally, **Communicate** the results of your research and targeting.

Many people who got their job through a speculative application often say it was a case of their CV hitting the right desk at the right time. This is only half the story: without the preliminary research and targeting, the right desk would never have been found and if you are well-informed of the circumstances of a company, the right time is easier to judge. This chapter considers how to:

- research and target the job
- research and target organizations
- target and communicate your application

> **!** ***Quick Tip: you have to be strong to make speculative applications***
>
> The success rate of speculative applications is low, and you need to keep this fact in mind, so that you do not take a potential string of rejections personally. If you are feeling disheartened by a difficult job search, it is probably best to steer clear of speculative applications until you are feeling positive.

Which job?

If you have followed the section on researching yourself in Chapter 2, you should have at least a rough idea of what type of job you want in what sector. However, finding the job that suits you if your knowledge of the sector is only hazy can be a problem. To pinpoint the role that would be ideal for you, try the following routes.

- Look at adverts in the sector and even if the particular job does not appeal, request the application pack. The job, company, and departmental descriptions will help you see what other positions there are. For example, a company structure diagram will show you all the departments and what roles they fulfil. You can then start to target the section within organizations where your career aims and skills are matched.
- Look at the staff and contact lists of company websites. The more informative websites will give an overall picture of each person's responsibilities. Note down which jobs most closely match your goals.
- The careers pages of newspaper websites (and hard print) often include interviews with people doing all sorts of jobs in all sorts of disciplines. These interviews frequently give details of how the person originally landed the job. Use their experience to help you both target the job and discover how they got into their role: can you follow a similar path?
- Look at adverts from recruitment agencies and make a list of those agencies which specialize in the sector you are most interested in.
- Attend careers fairs and seminars where larger employers will be on hand to discuss both recruitment procedures and the range of individual jobs they offer.

Keep a list of the job titles which match your aims so that you can quickly identify these in adverts.

You should also keep a list of the jargon used in your chosen sector so that you can use this in your application.

Which company?

Once you have defined the job, you need to research which company is most likely to be open to a speculative application. Here are some suggestions for identifying the right company:

- The Internet is the easiest and fastest way to research company information. Prepare a standard checklist of information to complete so that you don't forget any vital data, as shown in the example below, which Joe is using to research music companies.

FULL NAME OF COMPANY	*BEST NOISE MUSIC LTD*
ANY PARENT COMPANY? IF SO WHICH?	*JOHNSON MUSIC*
HEAD OFFICE ADDRESS	*25 East Street, Southampton SO2*
ADDRESS OF BRANCH I WOULD BE INTERESTED IN	*No branches*
TELEPHONE	*023 34983493*
EMAIL	*info@bestnoise.com*
WEBSITE ADDRESS	www.bestnoise.com (www.johnsonbeats.com)
NAME OF PERSON WHO DEALS WITH APPLICATIONS	*No name at Best Noise*
NAME OF HEAD OF DEPARTMENT I AM INTERESTED IN	*Don't seem to be departments at Best Noise*
COMPANY'S MISSION STATEMENT/SLOGAN	*'Making the best noise in the world'*
ADDITIONAL INFO ON MAIN BUSINESS	*Brings in new bands and brings them up to Johnson's level*
WHAT'S NEW? EXPANSIONS, NEW PRODUCTS	*Signed up 7 new groups whole of last year and have already signed 10 this year—expanding*

FULL NAME OF COMPANY	*BEST NOISE MUSIC LTD*
ANYONE WHOSE NAME I RECOGNIZE ON STAFF LIST	*I think Josh Miller, Administrator, was at school with me. Email and find out what he thinks of company!*
NEWS ON COMPANY FROM OTHER WEBSITES	*Lots of positive stuff on music magazine sites*
CAREERS SECTION OF WEBSITE?	*Best Noise says not taking applications till Jan. 2013*
DATE APPLICATION LETTER SENT	*15 January 2013*
RESPONSE	*Holding letter saying right person away on holiday: chase in 2 weeks' time*

Be careful how you chase: it can be irritating to a busy HR department.

Joe could also see if he can find out how many people there are on the staff. A common error people writing speculative applications make is not to realize that there may only be a very small staff (less than 10), in which case vacancies are rare, and speculative applications are even less successful than usual.

- Keep an eye on the financial section of national and local news websites to identify which companies are expanding and what new companies are being set up.
- Look in trade press publications for stories on organizations in the sector: who is expanding, who is seeking to fill gaps in their staff. Trade press publications often also carry news about staff moves which may indicate an opening for you but you will need to move quickly on these as the publication is probably running some way behind events.

!

Quick Tip: careers sections of websites

If the company has a vacancies or careers section on its website, make this your first port of call. These web pages will tell you if the company is interested in receiving applications at the current time and how to apply. Specific jobs will also be advertised. If the careers pages state that the company is not accepting applications for the present, respect this: you are wasting your time if you do not and the company will assume you did not take the trouble to check. You can, however, call the HR department and ask if there is a date in the future when applications will be accepted. Some departments will add you to their list of waiting candidates and advise you by email when they reopen the application process. Otherwise, make a note of the date you are given and try again then.

Target and communicate your application

A speculative application should consist of a covering letter and an up-to-date CV, each targeted at the company you are applying to. Your research on the job and the company should enable you to provide this focus. The following indicates what you should include in your covering letter.

Introduce yourself

A recruitment manager needs to know something about you straight away to be encouraged to read on through the rest of your letter. Hannah, writing to a local call centre, has begun her letter as follows:

I am writing to you to enquire if there are any vacancies within your customer care call centre team. Following a career break while my children were young, I am keen to restart my working life, building on my previous experience as a call centre supervisor.

> !
>
> ***Quick Tip: who to send your letter to***
>
> Find out the name of the person handling recruitment and address your letter to them. Do not send your application to the head of the department you want to join as companies generally have a policy of sending speculative applications straight to the HR or Personnel department.

Explain what you are looking for

This can be covered (as in the example with Hannah above) in the introduction to yourself. However, if you have stated that you are interested in 'financial' or 'operational' posts, you need to be more specific about what job you are interested in. Richard could write, for example:

I am interested in managerial posts, ideally connected with design and production issues.

The danger with being too specific about the job role you are interested in is that, if that role does not exist within the company or is already filled, you are writing yourself out of any possibility of a job. The alternative approach is demonstrated by what Joe writes to a music company:

As an enthusiastic college leaver with a real passion for the music industry and a range of basic office skills, I am interested in any posts where you think my talents would be useful to the company.

Explain why you have selected this company

This helps a recruitment manager to pinpoint what you are expecting from the company. You might say that the company is a market leader and you are keen to learn the benchmark standards of the industry. You could also focus on the company being new and young in its industry and your interest in being part of a growing and innovative business.

Demonstrate what you can bring to the company

This is a vital aspect of your letter. This harks back to the need to show why a company that did not know it needed you will be convinced that you should join the staff. Highlight your specific skills (such as communications, IT, similar work experience) which will be of real benefit to the company. Hannah writes in her letter:

I believe that several of my skills would be advantageous to the company:

- solid experience in a similar role
- first class telephone communication skills
- a total commitment to customer care standards: going the extra mile to achieve those standards and so raising the reputation of the company
- excellent at motivating a team and giving them pride in their work

It is important to be clear about your relevant skills and experience (especially if you are trying to change career path) so that an employer is not trying to pick out from your CV what might be helpful to the organization.

Besides the usual concluding remarks of any application letter (***see*** Chapter 4, the section, 'Answering any queries the application raises') you could finish with one or more of the following options:

- *offer to work voluntarily* if you are really keen to work for the company, or want to know if the job would be all that you believe. (***See also also*** the section on Apprentices and Interns later in this chapter.) Larger companies and charities will be open to this suggestion: the larger companies because they have the time and the staff resources to train and supervise a volunteer, charities because they are often understaffed. This is a useful approach if you are in the middle of changing careers. For example, Richard could write:

  I have limited experience in charities (several weeks' voluntary work) and would be very interested in taking on any voluntary work–whether in or out of the design and production department–to get a thorough grounding in how your own charity operates. Please do not feel that I would only be interested in managerial type work: I am very happy to work as part of a team or solo on any administrative project if this would be of use to the charity.

- *ask for your details to be kept on file* so that if there are no current vacancies you could be considered in the future. This happens more frequently than you might think. Recruitment managers are keen to have a 'bank' of potential candidates on whom they can call and so avoid advertising costs if possible.
- *ask for feedback* on your application, but don't expect always to get a response. Recruitment managers have many calls on their time though they will generally try to give you some pointers.

You could close your letter with a word about your preferred salary range, but make sure you have done your research carefully on what the going rate is. You can easily price yourself out of the market, or cast doubt on your ability by pitching too low. Giving a salary range of £5,000 avoids this potential problem, for example, Hannah writes:

I am looking for a salary in the range of £25,000 to £30,000 p.a.

!

Quick Tip: do you mean it?

Nothing is more irritating for a recruitment manager to receive an interesting spec letter, only to call the candidate and be put off by lack of enthusiasm or, worse, to be told that the person is no longer looking. Be courteous and inform the recruitment manager you are withdrawing your application for the time being: this can only help your reputation if you want to return to an application in the future.

Apprentices and interns

Apprenticeships and internships can be a useful way in to employment and give you an excellent grounding in general and sector-specific skills.

Apprenticeships are now available in many sectors beyond traditional engineering, construction, and skilled manual crafts: the performing arts, teaching, social care, law, and advisory organizations are just some of the diverse areas offering apprenticeships. Apprenticeships are mainly aimed at young adults aged 16–25, but the age range continues to expand and apprenticeships offer a useful route if you are trying to re-train for a different career.

Apprenticeships are paid positions, usually lasting at least 6 months and up to 3 years. The best apprenticeships will offer you some form of qualification or accreditation, either through training on the job or through partnerships with local colleges or training organizations. Sometimes a combination of both will be available.

You will find information about all aspects of apprenticeships at the National Apprenticeship Service's website: www.apprenticeships.org.uk. The website includes an apprenticeship matching service, with details of available places throughout the UK.

Internships tend to be aimed at graduates keen to gain experience in a specialized field: politics, law, media, and the arts are rich in intern opportunities but the range of internships is as wide as for apprenticeships, and they are available in health care, the charity sector, and information services. An internship generally lasts for between 3 and 6 months. You will usually be expected to have basic work skills: the internship is to give you a working insight into your chosen sector. This could be through working alongside an experienced member of staff, carrying out a project, working on a rotational basis with a number of departments.

The Internet has plenty of websites for finding internships, but you might want to start your search at Graduate Talent Pool, the government site, on http://graduatetalentpool.direct.gov.uk. As a comprehensive site offering posts in all areas, this is a useful starting point to give you ideas on what is available.

Internships and apprenticeships may be paid or unpaid. Internships have had a mixed press for this reason, as some employers have used them as a means of finding 'cheap labour'. Spot the better opportunities by asking what previous interns have moved on to and perhaps speaking to them personally. Ask how long an employer has run apprenticeships or internships: a new scheme is not necessarily a bad thing as you could have the opportunity to help train the company during your term, setting up a constructive scheme which benefits you, the company, and future interns/apprentices. However, you need to be confident that the employer is genuinely interested in running the scheme, not just paying lip service to a national or local authority initiative which brings money into the organization.

A good apprenticeship can be life changing. Here is what one apprentice, from The Reader Organisation in Liverpool, has to say about her experience:

> The one thing that I have noticed since starting at The Reader is that my confidence has grown so much and that I have continuous support with whatever I need help with, from when I moved into my flat to doing things I never thought I would be able to do, like doing training courses. I thought I would just crumble but I haven't. I'm grateful to have this opportunity as The Reader has changed my life.... For the better.

And, on the flip side of the coin, here is what the apprentice's manager has to say:

> Sitting on a panel interviewing 10 hopeful young people (many of them care leavers) for one apprenticeship was one of the hardest afternoons of my working life: so much promise, so much potential, such hard life lessons already learnt by those who put themselves forward. Managing the successful candidate–who was only 17 when she joined the Reader Organisation–has been a deeply rewarding experience and one of the key things we've learnt is that a holistic approach is crucial: pastoral care and personal development are closely intertwined with professional growth, especially when the young person in question is living alone, learning how to pay bills, manage a budget, and run a flat. Well-being at work–for our apprentices in particular–has to begin at home and as employers we're fully prepared to take that on board.

This is an example of the best type of modern apprenticeship–and there are many more such inspiring opportunities out there.

Summary of Main Points

1. Research the type of jobs which interest you through adverts, company staff lists, reading case studies of how people gained their job, attending careers fairs.
2. Research the type of company you are interested in, and construct an information database of the company's recruitment facts.
3. Target your covering letter and CV by using the research you have carried out.
4. Explain why you are writing, why you want to work for the company, and what skills/ experience you have which are relevant; what you can bring to the company.
5. Balance being specific about what type of post you are seeking with being general enough not to rule yourself out of potential opportunities.
6. Focus on the positive aspects of why you want to join the company, not an attractive salary!
7. Consider working voluntarily if you are passionate about gaining the skills and experience you think an organization can offer you.
8. Ask for your details to be kept on file, but don't forget to take your name off the waiting list if you find another post.
9. Check out apprenticeships and internships.
10. Be prepared for lots of rejections—and don't take them personally.

8 Interviews

CONTENTS

120
Introduction

120
Preparing for your interview

124
Different types of interview

131
Presenting yourself to your best advantage

133
Summary of main points

134
Congratulations... you've got the job!

Introduction

An interview is an essential part of every company's recruitment procedure. To get a job without an interview is highly unlikely, and you therefore need to assemble and develop a range of interview skills to back up your paper application.

The essential skills of interviewing involve the building blocks of **Prepare** and **Communicate**. You need to be ready to put your case as persuasively in speech as you have done on paper. A frequent complaint of recruitment managers is that candidates 'looked great on paper, but were so disappointing at interview'. Don't give up when you get to the interview stage—you are still within the application process.

You should remember that an interview is a two-way process. In a reversal of the situation above, a job that might have looked great on paper can be disappointing at interview. The recruitment manager must sell you the post as much as you sell yourself.

This chapter looks at:

- preparing for an interview
- different types of interview
- interview questions
- techniques to show yourself to your best advantage

Preparing for your interview

There is usually a time lapse between sending in your application for a job and hearing that you have an interview. In that time lapse you may well forget the details of the job description and what you wrote in your application. Your first tasks in preparing for an interview are therefore as follows.

- Re-read all the details about the job and the company which were sent to you and make notes of any points you would like clarified at the interview. You should aim to be able to state in a couple of sentences what the company does and what its main aims are. Look back over the research you did on the company and bring it up to date through Internet research on the company's website and any stories that might be reported on news websites.
- Re-read your own application and remember what you said were your reasons for applying; the experience and skills you cited as being relevant; any other points you included. If you present a totally different case for being the right person at the interview, the interviewer will be left with the impression that you are uncertain why you applied for the job. It is fine to *add* items to your case, but make them hang together with the rest of your presentation to give a logical argument.

Next you need to **interview yourself**. Practise giving a coherent description of your career from a variety of starting points (from leaving school, college, or university, over the past two, five, or ten years), emphasizing the parts which are most relevant to the job. Ask yourself why you want the job and build up an answer from the reasons you gave in your application.

You then need to think about questions that might be asked which are specific to this job. If you have stated that you have relevant skills, you will need to explain how you gained these and demonstrate how you use them at the moment. For example, if Richard has applied for a job which involves dealing with budgets, he would need to be ready to describe any formal or informal training, how he sets and manages a budget, and how he deals with any budgetary problems.

Interviewers will often pose a 'suppose that' type of question, wanting you to solve a standard situation that arises in the job. This could be dealing with a difficult customer, deciding how to prioritize multiple tasks, working with different types of people, dealing with deadlines. To give your answer the edge, try to think how you could include an example of how you have dealt with similar situations in past or present jobs. An interviewer might ask Kashmira how she would deal with an underperforming member of the team (a favourite management question). Kashmira would need to make some suggestions on how to motivate the employee and preferably refer to an experience with her current team when she has resolved a similar situation.

You should then prepare answers to questions which might be asked about your personal situation. If Hannah is asked how she feels about returning to work after a long break, she could think about constructing an answer showing that she has continued the discipline of work during the break by gaining an additional qualification or helping a friend with work at home. Kashmira might be asked to explain why she wants to move from a job in Manchester to a job in London and needs an answer on how she will cope with relocating and extra living costs. Your answers show the employer you have thought through the 'side issues' of working with their company and can deal with them.

Quick Tip

Don't feel you should always try to give conciliatory answers on staff questions: it is fine to display your 'tough' side too by showing that you can put your foot down and control a team—constructively—too.

Finally, you need to think about your interests and hobbies. Informal interviews will often involve finding out more about you as a person, so you should be ready to talk about the things you enjoy doing outside work. For example, Joe needs to be ready to talk about how his football club is doing this season, and which recent music releases he thinks are good.

Once you are reasonably confident about your answers, ask a friend or relative to go through some standard questions with you. There are two purposes to this: you will get a chance to give your answers to someone and hear how you sound, while your friend or relative can give you honest feedback.

Quick Tip

Don't over-rehearse your answers. You could be left floundering if an expected question is framed in a different way: your rehearsed answer needs to have enough flexibility to suit the question that is actually being asked. If you fail to listen to the question and reply with facts that are not what the interviewer wanted, you could be marked down on your skills in listening and attention to detail.

Technical preparation

There are some 'technical' preparations you should also carry out in good time.

- Check the interview invitation and see if you have been asked to bring anything (CV, portfolio of work). Have it ready by the night before the interview.

- Have a street map ready to take with you: the interviewing company will usually provide directions if you ask, if they do not send a map with the interview details. Work out how long the journey will take—perhaps even doing a dummy run. You should allow at least an extra fifteen minutes for the journey, in case something goes wrong.
- Take the phone number of the company with you so if something does go wrong on the way to the interview, you can ring and explain.
- Check what you are going to wear and don't leave it to the last minute to find your best suit is at the cleaners. You should always dress smartly and formally for a first interview. For a second interview, take your cue from the first time round, but do not drop below the level of 'smart casual'.

Interview nerves

Everyone gets nervous before an interview. There are some things you can do to stop yourself being overwhelmed by nerves.

- Follow the preparation list above.
- Allow yourself enough time to get to the interview and to have five minutes to sit and wait: arriving out of breath and flustered does not help interview nerves and will create a poor first impression.
- Remember that the company would not have asked you to an interview if they didn't think you could do the job.
- Take your time in answering questions. If you are asked something you have not thought about before, it is perfectly acceptable to say, 'That's a tough/interesting/different one. Let me just think about that for a moment.'
- Ignore other interviewees who sit beside you and say, 'I hear they're really tough'. Sadly there are some people who like to increase their chances by demoralizing other candidates.
- Smile when you meet your interviewers! Smiling relaxes all your facial muscles, and it also establishes an instant rapport with the interviewing panel.

Different types of interview

All interviews consist of three standard elements:

- **introductions:** you will be introduced to the interviewers by name and perhaps by job title and given a brief description of what they do. Experienced interviewers will also 'introduce' you to the job and the company, explaining in more detail any information sent to you as part of the application. Interviewers often use this section of the interview to give you time to settle your nerves: they know that you may not take everything in at this point, but you do need to stay alert and pick up any items that you may want to ask questions about later on (for example, why the current postholder is leaving). Your final introduction may be to meet the people with whom you would be working and to be taken round the office to get a general feel for where you would be working.
- **questions to you:** *see* the next section for more details.
- **questions from you:** your opportunity to clarify any points which are not made clear during the interview—training and career prospects, the company's plans over the next year to three years, why the previous postholder left or, if this is an entirely new post, the size of the team and its structure.

There are now many different ways for companies to interview candidates from the traditional face-to-face to Skype interviews. If you are faced with a type of interview you have not participated in previously, it really is worth taking time to do some research so that your interview nerves are not increased by wondering what is going to happen next.

Face-to-face interviews

A well-organized company will tell you when you are invited to interview how many people—and who—will be at your interview. Ask for this information if you are not given it automatically: it can be off-putting if you were expecting one interviewer and are suddenly presented with a panel of six. Check out company literature or the website to put the people you will be meeting in their organizational context. For example, is this the person to whom you will be responsible, a manager from a different department, or a team member? Managers from different departments are often used to interview candidates to give a consistent approach in staff recruitment across a company.

Face-to-face interviews can be very formal affairs, perhaps involving facing a board of interviewers on one side of a table with you on the other. In this situation the rule is to try and include everyone in your answers, by looking round at them and not fixing merely on the person in front of you. These interviews are used for more senior posts. Face-to-face interviews may also be quite informal events, with the atmosphere of having a chat with one or more people. Recruitment managers will use this approach when they are looking for someone who will fit into the team or if it is a small company where personality will count as much as skill and experience.

Telephone interviews

Companies may use an initial telephone interview to filter candidates for a post where many applications are expected. Adverts will usually say something along the lines of 'for an initial exploratory conversation, call this number'. Make your call from a quiet, private location where you will not be interrupted and cannot be overheard. Do not make a call on your mobile phone if you are on the move as background noise and possible cut outs will not help your chances. You will probably be asked to give a brief rundown of your career and skills to date and be asked a couple of questions on availability and salary. If you are surprised by a company calling to ask if they can talk to you over the phone and it is not a convenient time (if you are in an open plan office, for example), ask if you can call the person back at a given time and arrange to make the call privately.

Assessment centres

Assessment centres may be run by the company which you are applying to, or by an external company which is recruiting for the company. They are used for longer interview sessions, lasting at least the whole of one day and often several days. The process at an assessment centre may consist of presentations by the company and different departments, a number of face-to-face interviews, psychometric tests, role plays, and team exercises. Companies use assessment centres to gain an accurate picture of candidates in whom they expect to invest a good deal of training and development. Judging potential (rather than current experience and skills) is therefore vital and takes longer than a standard interview.

Skype or video-conferencing interviews

Employers are making increasing use of Skype and other webcam and video-conferencing services to carry out interviews, especially if the organization is multinational: it is obviously much cheaper to interview on Skype than fly you to New York or Munich. For the interview, you may be invited to the offices of the potential employer, or to a third party organization providing the service. However, if you have your own Skype service, you may be interviewed at home.

When you are interviewed in this way, remember that the interviewer can *see* you. It is too easy to forget this simple point, and there are many stories by both interviewers and interviewees of embarrassing and funny moments—such as interviewees still in pyjamas, having all too obviously just staggered out of bed. If you are being interviewed at home, check what background your webcam will pick up and try to make it as neutral as possible, so your interviewer is not distracted by posters, empty wine bottles or discarded clothing. If you live with other people, tell them when your interview is taking place and ask them to keep noise levels low and not interrupt you.

Tests

Many organizations use some form of testing to check out specific skills (IT, spelling, maths), potential for development (psychometric and personality tests, role play, and mock presentations) to filter candidates. The company *should* tell you when inviting you for interview if any tests will be held, but it is worth asking if there will be a test of any kind if this is not mentioned in the invitation.

These tests are not exams so you should not get over-anxious about them; if you do not reach the standard the company is looking for, then the job is not right for you. However, you should prepare in advance to make sure you do yourself justice. Look for tests available to try over the Internet, especially those which can be downloaded and kept for future use. There are also plenty of books containing examples of tests to try out at your leisure.

Second interviews

Second interviews are held for two reasons.

- The first interview filters out most candidates, leaving a short list to be reinterviewed at greater length, perhaps by different managers. This technique is used where managers can only spend a limited amount of time interviewing, so they only want to see candidates who are definitely suitable. This often happens where the recruitment process is being handled by an agency. Your first interview will be with the agency, the second with the organization itself.
- Candidates are so closely matched that the interviewers need another conversation with them to make a final decision. Different interviewers may be used, to get a different perspective.

If you are invited to a second interview, think back to your first interview and consider any hints you picked up about the type of person the company is looking for and skills that seemed especially important. How can you emphasize these?

Interview questions

Fools ask questions that wise men cannot answer.

Traditional proverb

What precise questions you are asked at interview will depend on the job you are applying for. You can roughly guess and prepare for what will be asked by considering what things are likely to crop up under the following headings.

ABOUT THE JOB

- Why do you want the job?
- What makes you the right person for the job?
- What will be your main contribution to this job?
- How would you start this job?

Break answers to questions of this sort down into sections:

- your personal interest: how the job matches your career intentions and what appeals to you personally about it;
- corresponding experience: the parallels with experience gained from previous and current jobs;
- skills you have already which are needed for the job.

By giving your answer this structure, you can check that you are covering all the points that are important, and give your interviewer a format to follow.

ABOUT YOUR CAREER

- What are you doing at the moment?
- What job did you enjoy most/least and why?
- Why did you leave each job?
- What are your career plans?

You should be able to answer in one or two sentences each of these questions and make it relevant to the job you are applying for now. For example, if Joe was answering the career plan question he could answer:

I would like to keep all my options open right now as I don't have enough experience in different roles and companies to have a really well planned career, and this is why this job appeals to me, as you are asking for someone to take on a range of tasks–just what I need to give me an idea of all the things I could do and then be able to concentrate on the one that suits me best.

This phase of the interview is also an opportunity for you to fill in any gaps in your career history or explain any changes.

Ideally, when explaining why you left each post, you should be able to say that you wanted to develop your career, but as this is often not the case, you may need to add some extra explanation. If you lost a job through no fault of your own (such as redundancy) and followed this up with temporary work or a sideways move into a new career, it is fine to say so. For example, Hannah could explain that, although she started out as a secretary in a law firm, her job was made redundant when her firm merged with another. She took on her first customer service role as a stop gap while looking for another legal secretary job, but liked customer service so much she has stayed in it ever since.

If your last job came unstuck, you need to plan the answer to what happened carefully, asking yourself honestly what was the reason. What will be different about this job? Have you resolved the personal problems which caused the upset? Have you sorted out why you had a personality clash with your colleagues or manager? Have you realized that you were just plain bored by the job? If any of these apply to you, you could base your answer round the following example:

My last job came to an end because I had a lot of personal problems at the time–my wife and I were splitting up and I'm afraid the job took a very low priority. But I can now confidently say that that is in the past: I've enjoyed the temporary work I've done since then and that has given me the chance to realize this is the job/area I should be in.

Quick Tip

If you are not in work, give some examples of how you are keeping 'work disciplined' at the interview: working part time, voluntary work, etc.

ABOUT YOUR SKILLS

- Which skills are relevant to this job?
- What extra skills do you have?
- Which skills do you like most?
- Which skills are you missing?

You should target your answer and give a measure of what level you are at with the particular skill. For example:

I have all the IT skills you require on the job description and I have advanced skills in Dreamweaver and Oracle.

If you don't have a particular skill, show your grasp first of a similar skill and secondly your ability to learn a skill by describing how you learnt something recently. For instance, Richard is asked at interview what skill he has in MS Project. He could reply:

We didn't use MS Project at my last company, but we used a package which I hear is quite similar–Bloggs Plan. I hadn't used it before I went to the company, but found it very simple to pick up and I found that this type of software back up to a project is very helpful.

ABOUT YOU

- What are your strengths?
- What are your weaknesses?
- Are you ambitious?
- What are your interests?

Your answers to these questions are the stage of the interview when you need to draw on what you have picked up about the job and the company both from your pre-interview research and from the interview so far. If the interviewer is obviously looking for a team player, stress your team skills. Conversely, if you went into interview believing that this was a role for a team player but have realized since then that this is a post requiring someone to work with a team but have their own responsibilities which will not be shared by the rest of the team, you would need to modify your answer.

Questions on your personality ('Are you ambitious?') can be traps if you do not think about them carefully. The temptation is to become introspective and ramble, which is not what is required. Your personality in relation to the job and the organization is what is important rather than your personality outside work.

Your interests are a good point for an interviewer to get a real conversation going with you. Be up to date with your interests so if you have listed reading as a favourite hobby, be ready to talk about the book you are reading now and what you enjoyed most over the past year. You should still be a little wary: if you give the impression that you are out clubbing until 3 a.m. every morning, an interviewer will have doubts as to your alertness at work at 9 a.m.

RECORDING YOUR INTERVIEW

Keep a log of the interviews you attend, especially if there is to be a second interview. You then have a point of reference to start your preparation for the next time round.

Keep a note of any questions you were asked which you have not come across before and think how you could have answered them differently or better for the future. Here is Joe's record of an interview:

COMPANY NAME	*BIG NOISE MUSIC*
POST	*GENERAL ADMINISTRATOR*
DATE OF INTERVIEW	*2 DECEMBER 2012*
INTERVIEW VENUE	*42 EAST STREET, SOUTHAMPTON (NB THE ENTRANCE WAS IN LITTLE STREET!)*
WHO INTERVIEWED AND THEIR POSITION IN COMPANY	*MARCUS DIGBY—PROMOTIONS MANAGER, HELEN ABER—OFFICE MANAGER*
WHAT DID THEY ASK	• *WHAT I KNEW ABOUT THE COMPANY* • *WHAT MUSIC I LIKED* • *WHY I WANTED TO WORK FOR BIG NOISE (SAID PERSONAL INTEREST, GOOD SKILLS MATCH)* • *HOW I COPE WITH DIFFICULT PEOPLE, DEADLINES, PRESSURE* • *HOW FAST I LEARNED NEW SOFTWARE*
WHAT WENT WELL	*LIKED THE PEOPLE; THOUGHT I ANSWERED QUESTIONS WELL; THEY SHOWED ME ROUND*
WHERE I COULD IMPROVE	• *GOT THERE LATE BECAUSE OF THE ENTRANCE IN THE OTHER STREET!* • *DIDN'T FEEL HAD ENOUGH QUESTIONS TO ASK THEM*
ANY TESTING	*SHORT TEST ON OPENING UP THE INTERNET, FINDING WEBSITES FOR TWO GROUPS AND THEN INFO ON THEIR LATEST RELEASES. NO PROBLEMS.*
WHEN COMPANY IS TO CONTACT ME	*BY 10 DECEMBER*
FEEDBACK	*SECOND INTERVIEW 12 DECEMBER! WILL BE WITH MARCUS DIGBY AND SARAH JOHNSON (HR MANAGER OF PARENT COMPANY)*

Presenting yourself to your best advantage

Interviews are the sum total of a number of things: answers, aptitude and attitude. Interviewers are looking for someone who will be a real benefit to the company. Just as you would not buy an expensive item without careful thought, a company will not want to pay someone a fair proportion of its income without considering all the aspects of that person.

Body language

Sitting up, alert and attentive to the people who are interviewing you, will create a much better impression that if you slump in your seat gazing at the floor. Be aware of the image you are presenting.

Asking questions

Do not feel you have to have a battery of intelligent and fascinating questions to ask. If the interviewer is experienced, most of the points you thought to ask will probably have been covered already. It is fine to say, 'Actually no, because you've answered them all already! But is there anything I've said that gives you any concern about whether I'm suitable for the job?'

Stating your interest

Do always say at an appropriate point in the interview how much the job interests you. You could say this when you are asked if you have any questions. Expanding on the example above, you could say, 'Actually no, because you've answered them all already! But is there anything I've said that gives you some concerns about whether I'm suitable for the job, because I believe I would really enjoy doing it?'

Stand out from the crowd

Can you find something different or funny to say which will mark you out from other candidates? Interviewing six equally matched graduates at one time, I selected the one who said with absolute sincerity, 'Yes, I would love this job: please save me from being in the rat race!' His sense of humour was exactly what we needed in the team and he was appointed.

Quick Tip

If your interview was arranged by an agency, always ring and tell them how it went and if there were any unexpected items such as tests or a large interview panel. Agencies do the best they can, but sometimes the company hiring them doesn't tell them what the interview will contain.

Summary of Main Points

1. Prepare for your interview by re-reading the job description, any other information the organization sent you and your application.
2. Check the Internet for the latest news on the organization.
3. Interview yourself to rehearse answers which you think you could be asked, but don't be too prescriptive to save you getting stuck if the question is not framed in the way you expect.
4. Ask a friend or family member to practise the interview with you.
5. Prepare for the nuts and bolts of the interview in good time: anything you were asked to bring; a map and transport instructions; clothes to wear.
6. If you are not told who will be interviewing you, ask. Check what their role is from the information you have been given or researched.
7. Ask if there will be any skills tests and practise for them.
8. If you are being interviewed on Skype, check your IT and ensure that the room you are using (if at home) presents a neutral background.
9. Keep a record of the interview for use in the future: what questions were asked and could you have given a better answer?
10. Remember the three As: answers, aptitude, and attitude.

Congratulations...you've got the job!

What happens next

The offer of a job is usually made by phone, so make sure you can be reached easily after the interview. The employer will want to discuss with you the details of starting date and salary, plus perhaps employee benefits. Once these are agreed, the employer will be able to send you an offer letter, which forms the contract between you. The letter should confirm:

- job title
- starting date
- starting salary (and any bonus or commission arrangements)
- pension: all employers are required to give employees access to a pension scheme
- probationary period
- holiday entitlement
- sick leave arrangements
- employee benefits: for example private medical care, life insurance, critical illness insurance, gym membership, season ticket loans. Usually these are not available until you have successfully completed the probationary period.

The job offer may be made subject to:

- satisfactory references. You may like to contact your referees to let them know that your prospective employer will be contacting them
- evidence of any qualifications, such as A-level and degree certificates
- attending a medical examination if you are in a key position. If you have a disability, this will be taken into account
- proof of your right to work in the UK (***see*** 'Additional questions' in Chapter 5).

The employer will probably send two copies of the offer letter. You sign both and return one copy to the employer, retaining the other for your own records.

The offer letter may also refer to full Terms & Conditions being given to you when you start work. These will include items such as the company policy on discrimination, use of social media (companies can be very sensitive to remarks made by employees on such sites), disciplinary and grievance procedures. You can ask the employer for a copy of these if you want to check these before you accept the offer.

The day you start work, you will be asked for your P45, which will tell the employer what tax code you are on and affects what tax will be deducted from your pay. If your previous employer has yet to issue your P45, or this is your first job, you will be put on an 'emergency tax code' until the tax office lets the employer know what the correct code is.

If you didn't ask for a copy of the full Terms and Conditions of employment, these should be given to you within one month of starting work. It really is important to read these through, otherwise you may find that you have broken a requirement without knowing why—or that the employer is not fulfilling its side of the arrangement.

Some employers also have an 'employee handbook', which could include not only the Terms and Conditions, but also the company's standard practices of working, which cover everything from dress code to who loads the dishwasher. Again, do take the time to read through these to ensure you don't inadvertently annoy your colleagues by doing—or not doing—something in the accepted way.

You will probably go through an induction period, when you will be trained in how to do your job. This may be a formal training, with set sessions and ongoing checks on your progress, or more informal, with training happening as you perform your work. It is important to keep asking questions and keep asking for extra help to enable you to gain the grounding you need in the basic tasks of your role.

At the end of your probationary period, you will probably have a meeting with your line manager to discuss how you each feel your work is progressing and to identify any additional training needs. Targets for the next six to twelve months may also be set, to be reviewed at set times.

Salary

Your salary may be paid weekly or monthly, and employers prefer to make payment direct to a bank account. If you do not have an account already, take your job offer letter to the bank of your choice and ask them about setting up an account.

You are entitled to be given a pay slip each time your salary is paid, which will give details of tax and National Insurance (plus any other deductions). Do check your pay slips and ensure you raise any queries you have at the first opportunity.

Finally, well done for getting the job. I hope that you have found this book helpful, and I wish you every success with your career.

Troubleshooting

9

CONTENTS

137
Introduction

Nice work if you can get it, And you can get it if you try.

Ira Gershwin

Introduction

All careers have a tendency to hit problems somewhere along the line. You may fall out with colleagues, you may be made redundant, you may feel stuck in a rut, you might feel as if your job applications never lead anywhere. This chapter deals with some of the problems that crop up when making a job application.

I apply for plenty of jobs but I never seem to get an interview

Applying for lots of jobs may be the reason why you are not being successful in getting to the interview stage. You need to focus your efforts rather than sending out your CV to every job that looks interesting or which you think you could do. Make a list of all the job adverts which you want to apply to and then prioritize them. Apply for your top five first—which is five days' work. An application should take you a day to write, as you will need to target your CV and covering letter to make it relevant to each job.

Think about the following questions as well. Have you researched yourself and the job properly—are you applying for posts which are not suitable for you? Have you written a CV which is simple to read and focuses on the role? Are you leaving out vital content such as dates and skills? If you are changing career direction, have you explained this? Are you applying for an apparently lower/upper grade post without explaining why? Are you making it easy to be contacted?

Quick Tip

At the end of each job application, analyse what you did and where you think you could have improved. Ask a friend or family member to help you–but ask them to take an unbiased view: being friend or family they may try to be too optimistic to be helpful.

If you still get nowhere with applications, start ringing the companies you apply to and ask for feedback. Personnel managers are usually sympathetic to people keen to find work and will give you helpful advice. Listen to and act on their advice.

I've been to plenty of interviews, but these don't turn into job offers

Your interview technique may be letting you down. Ask for feedback from the companies you go to for interviews and be prepared for some home truths. Do not be defensive or offended, but listen to what is said to you and think how you can change your interview style. Ask friends and family to run through a mock interview with you and give you their honest opinion. If you are getting interviews through a recruitment agency, ask the agency for help. You could also look out for interview skills workshops being run by colleges and your local authority: your local library should be able to assist with details of these.

If you are confident that your technique is right, then you need to think about what you are saying at the interview. Are you, in effect, living up to what you say on your CV? If you claim to be knowledgeable about, for example, budgets and financial matters on your CV, but are unable to answer the interview questions, then you will need to rethink the way you have written your CV and whether you are applying for the right kind of job.

Finally, you need to consider if you are pricing yourself out of your particular job market. If you are consistently asking for more than other candidates, then you are unlikely to obtain a job offer. Recheck the going rate for the job from friends in similar roles and other adverts. Avoid using Internet salary surveys, which tend to be aimed at the high end of the scale and can only provide generalized salary advice.

How do I make my CV more interesting?

A bland, cover-all CV is guaranteed to get you nowhere. However, resist the temptation to use a jazzy design (unless you are applying for a design post) to boost your CV, and concentrate on the content. Keep to the rules:

- make it relevant through research and targeting;
- make it short, even cutting down to one side of A4.

Use language to liven up your CV without allowing it to ramble away from the point. Using positive, action words to describe your skills, experience, and achievements helps take your CV out of the general run and make it more confident. Examples are: 'first-class IT skills', 'four years' solid experience of customer service', 'met and exceeded sales targets', 'enjoy the challenge of a pressured environment', 'like to become actively involved in staff activities'.

Don't forget to use your interests section as a way of interesting the reader. 'Charity parachuting' or 'county tiddly winks champion' will always be more entertaining and attractive to a recruitment manager than 'watching television'.

Warning!

Don't overdo the self-marketing and ambitious aspect of your CV, unless you are applying for a post in a company which has a reputation for its staff being aggressively competitive. In most cases, HR managers will be looking for a team player rather than a team rival.

I never seem to have the right level of experience for the job

This is a very frustrating situation to be in. When you start out it can seem impossible to find a job, because everyone demands experience, while later on if you want to change direction, employers can be scared off by your being over-qualified. There are two approaches to resolving this situation.

- Turn your lack of experience or over-qualification into an asset in your covering letter. Here's what a management consultant does when faced with the situation:

I can sell my lack of experience as a strength because I have no preconceptions or prejudices, I can bring fresh ideas, and am eager to learn more.

I can sell my over-qualified experience as a strength because I bring a wealth of practical experience coupled with pragmatism based on a level of maturity that few others can offer.

You do need to match this approach to the job. A company looking for an office junior will not be tempted by an over-qualified person, nor will an employer looking for a team supervisor be convinced by a college leaver.

- Look for ways to increase your experience through voluntary work, odd jobs for friends and family. Whatever you do will always become useful at some point in your career.

Job searching in a time of recession

It's a recession when your neighbour loses his job; it's a depression when you lose yours.

Harry S. Truman (1884–1972), *Observer*

Finding your first job, trying to progress or losing your job through redundancy are the most difficult phases of a career, and these become even more difficult in times of economic crisis. The following are suggestions to mitigate the worst and give yourself the best chance.

Keeping fit

In the same way as you stay physically fit through exercise and a good diet, stay work fit by:

- creating and maintaining a work timetable for the week which includes job research, writing applications, and making appointments (and keeping them) for volunteering and training opportunities.
- keeping motivated through being part of a group in the same situation as yourself. Check with your local community centre, Jobcentre Plus, and other agencies for job clubs. If there isn't one, think of joining

with friends to start one for yourselves–and this could be online if your friends are not close by, as often happens after university or college, or if an organization for which you have all worked shuts down. Set a time when you will all log in to a social media page or other resource and set guidelines to keep the session to discussing and sharing what job research and applications you have each done, what your plans are for the next week, news you have about opportunities that could help the others in the group (even if they are not of interest to you). You could also set each other challenges such as drafting answers to questions which have cropped up on application forms or at interviews. If you find a job, help the rest of the group to stay motivated by continuing to send in thoughts on job search skills. You could also introduce someone else to the group when you leave to bring new ideas in and to keep up the numbers (as it can be very hard if you're the last person left in).

- maintaining and enhancing your work skills: basic skills, such as IT, need an occasional brush-up to stay up to date and ensure you are ready for any tests. You could use the time you are not in work to build on these skills, such as learning a new IT program, bookkeeping, or improving your language skills (in English or another language).
- research on the Internet and in trade press publications. Doing this will help you feel connected to and part of your industry.

All the above suggestions can be done at relatively low cost. Your local library can provide general IT and Internet access, and will also have details of local training courses. The library will also have a range of newspapers and magazines: if it does not currently take your trade magazine, you can ask for it be stocked (though whether this can be arranged may depend on general demand and the library's budget). Information about local free and subsidized training courses will be available at the library. Check out your local community centre too for the help it can provide in training, job clubs, or simply space to meet regularly with your group.

Do take advantage of every resource that is available to you in job searching. People are often very reluctant to contact, or even distrustful of, services that are available such as Jobcentres and other national or local authority initiatives. However, these services can only improve if people use them and give helpful feedback to the service. If you are a graduate, don't forget your university's graduate career service and other alumni services.

Thinking differently

In difficult economic times, you may well need to rethink your career plan and look for a compromise interim solution. Thinking differently about what you want to do can increase your options.

Volunteering has been referred to regularly throughout this book as a way of enhancing your skills and gaining work experience. A volunteering role–or even a number of roles–can make a major difference to you (and others) in a time of worklessness. You can use existing skills, gain new ones, make friends, and create a new support network to keep you motivated and upbeat. It can also point you in a different career direction to the one you had in mind–so do keep an open mind. Check the Internet for volunteering opportunities in your area, or sign up to one of the registers of volunteers also available on the Internet. Again, your library and local community centre can help you find volunteering places. If there is nothing advertised that appeals to you, think about local charities and services in which you are interested and write to them direct, with your CV, saying you are interested in volunteering and ask for their advice. The 'best' volunteering positions will give you the opportunity to gain an accreditation–for example in social care, the arts, advice–but if not, having a fixed point in your week when you are working can make a big impact on your motivation, self-confidence, and self-esteem.

Part-time work can sometimes be overlooked if you concentrate only on seeking a full-time role. But part-time, fixed-term and maternity cover contracts are all useful, and sometimes these types of posts can become permanent–especially if you perform particularly well. You can also build a portfolio of part-time posts, or a mixture of part-time paid work and a volunteering role. This can be a useful way of keeping a career aim alive if you can volunteer in your chosen sector and find another role which, besides paying the bills, keeps you up to scratch with basic work skills and a work ethos.

Looking beyond your area: can you consider jobs that are further afield? Accommodation is usually the main problem in this situation, but if you have family or friends who can give you a room, that is a starting point. Jobs which are outside your immediate area but within travelling distance could be another possibility, but you will need to think about the cost of travel. Consider car-sharing schemes or low-cost moped-hire projects, if public transport is not a viable answer.

You could also think about **self-employment**. Can you spot a niche in the local market which you could fill? Childcare, gardening, odd jobs are all standard favourites but there may be other gaps in the market you identify. Sustainability, healthy living, and 'green' issues are all current trends, and you may find there are local grants to help you get started in one of these fields.

In all these possible solutions, you need to use the blocks of **Research**, **Target**, and **Communicate**. Research the possibilities, target your approach to the organizations in which you are interested, and communicate what you can bring to an organization. Stay focused, stay motivated, and there will be a job for you.

I am worried about the reference I will get from my last company

If you fell out with your last employer, getting a reference can be a concern. However, under employment legislation, an employer providing a poor reference must be able to prove their criticism. A number of legal cases have made many companies reluctant to give a reference if the employee was unsatisfactory but no disciplinary action was taken and the employee left of their own accord. Alternatively, the employer may decide to give a bare, factual reference, merely stating the dates of employment and the job that was held.

The other point to remember is that you are not obliged to cite your manager as the person to give a reference: if you worked for a company with an HR department, you can direct reference enquiries to the HR department. This is useful if you had a personality clash with your manager but otherwise the job was fine. You could also cite other managers with whom you worked well.

If you were dismissed from your last post you do have a problem. The first thing is to get back into the job market as soon as possible through casual work and asking friends and family to give you work. You will then have one solid work reference to start building on. You would still need to explain what may seem to be a retrograde step in your career (e.g. change of tack, getting back to work after a break, looking for a less stressful post).

Although the press often carries stories about employers not checking references, the majority do, so don't be tempted to give false information: if you are caught out you could end up in an even greater muddle than before.

How I love a colleague-free day! Then I can really get on with the job.

Hugh Dalton (1887–1962), diary

I've had several changes of career direction: how will this affect my chances?

It all depends how you approach it in your CV and covering letter. Do not give too much prominence to past careers other than to emphasize any transferable skills which you can 'carry forward' into your next career. Group together jobs in an industry sector which you have now left behind, as discussed in Chapter 3.

Your covering letter (***see*** Chapter 4) should explain why you have decided to make your new career change and why you think this phase will last: employers will be doubtful about employing someone who only lasts six months in one career.

If you do find yourself constantly chopping and changing from one type of role to another, you probably do need to spend some time on deciding just what it is that you want to do. Look again at the section, 'Researching yourself' in Chapter 2 of this book: are you being honest with yourself about your interests and capabilities, or are you being too influenced by outside factors?

My questions always sound so dull when an interviewer asks me if I have anything to ask

You should certainly try to avoid 'filler' questions about when the company was established and how many employees there are—these are points that should have been covered in your own research about the organization. You should also avoid asking about salary and benefits until the interviewer raises this question, as you may sound as if you are more interested in the benefits than the job.

Look instead at the larger aspects of the role and the company. If not already covered at interview, ask what the employer wants the role to achieve over the next one to five years, and then move on to where that fits into the company aims for the next one to five years. You could also ask about the culture and 'feel' of the company: what opportunities are there for staff to have a say in policy? How long is the average length of service of staff? Would the interviewer describe the company as structured or informal?

Do not feel that you must ask lots of questions: two to three questions from posts below senior management level are plenty.

Index

Note; **major topics** and **reference** definitions are shown in **bold.**

abbreviations 21–24
academic/educational qualifications 39, 46, 52, 53, 54, 55, 75,
detail in **46,** 79, 89
academic CVs **65–66**
addresses 39
advertisements 16,
Internet **26–31,** 111
language used 21–25
recruitment managers and 80, 96
agencies **28**
see also consultancies; recruitment agencies
annual reports/accounts **32**
application forms 1, **87–99**
online **100–109**
application packs 16–17, 21, 31, 33
apprenticeships **117–118**
assessment centres 20, **125–126**

body language **132**
British Psychological Society 17
building blocks, *see* Communicate; Prepare; Research; Target

career history **40–45,** 48, 52, 54, 68, 101
developing **43–45**
unexpected moves 102
career structure **10–11**
careers **128–129**
aims 8, **10–11**, **12–14**, 28, 90, 111
aspirations 15
breaks in **44**, **45**, 72
changes in 8, 13, **144**
core skills in broad area of 10
fairs and seminars 111
'ideal' 11
checklists 112, **107**
clues 25, 34
hidden 19
Communicate (building block) **6, 38,** 70, 87, 110, 120
communication skills 12, 13, 115
community centre 104, 140, 141
company structure **32,** 111
computers, *see* email; Internet; online applications; software programs; web sites; word-processing
consultancies 15, 28
contacts 14
see also details
covering letters **21, 70–86, 114–116**
online applications **101, 105–106**, 114–116
criminal convictions/ Criminal Records Bureau 51, 94
current studies/situation **46,** 52, 54, **71**, 79
CVs (curricula vitae) **1, 17, 38–69,** 71, 100,137, **139, 144**
online **105–107**
templates 68
writing training 15

details
contact **39,** 51, 78
educational qualifications **46,** 79, 89
irrelevant 70
job/company 121
personal 51, 53, 116
disability **77**, 79
Disclosure and Barring Service **51**
dress 123
driving licence **46**

education **46,** 52
see also academic/educational qualifications
email 105–109
employment terms and conditions **135**
example applicants 2
experience 8, 9, 11, 13, 17, **38, 42, 55, 63, 90, 115, 116, 128,**
additional **73–75**
checking by agency 28

experience (contd)
demonstrating **73**
essential 87
lack of 140
relevant 121
right level of 139–140
suitable 102

face-to-face interviews **124–125**
false claims 42
family members 14, 94, 109, 138
feedback 15, 116, 122, 138
first aid **48**
first impressions 123
fonts 67, 80
freelance CV **57–58**
friends 14, 31, 35, 108, 109, 138

handwriting **36–37,** 97
head-hunting 28, 31
health 95
'hinterland' **22, 40**
humour 72, 132

induction period 135
information
company **19, 31–33, 75**
department **19**
essential **38–45**
organizational 20
specific **45–49**
initiative 34, 40, 40
internships **117–118**
interests 9, 12**, 13, 40,** 46, 52, 54, hobbies and 122, 130
Internet **26–30,** 34, 35, 111
see also web sites
searching **26–30**
interviews 1, 33, 37, 72, **122–136**
applicant unsuccessful in **137–138**
circumstances affecting attendance at 77
irrelevant 28
one of the most popular questions 8
panel 20
second 127
Skype and video conferencing interviews 126
technical preparation **122**
workshops on 15

jargon 72, 25, 41
job application process flowchart **4–5**
job club 35, 140, 141
job descriptions **16, 17,** 41, 43, 47, 75, 89, 90
reworded/rewritten 41
with notes **18–19**
job hunt 6
easier end of 110
job offers 134–5
job sharing **22–23**

knowledge 13, 33, 75
hazy 111
working 47, **24, 96**

language **21–24**
foreign **47**
making language work for you 25, 41, 72, 74, 79, 98, 106,
libraries 30, 35, 104, 107, 141, 142
LinkedIn 30

marital status **45**
mission statements 32
mistakes 50–51, 98–99
multiple posts **48**

names
applicant **38**
job **16**
referee **49**
National Insurance number 92, 95
nerves **123**, 124
networking 31
news articles **35, 113**
news websites 29
newsletters **33**
newspapers 29, 31
career sections 111
financial pages 113
notice period 78
online applications **100–109**
opportunities:
current 28
equal 96

over-exaggeration/overdo 42, 139
over-qualification 140

P45 135
part-time posts **24, 48**, 53, 78, 79
performing arts CVs **59–63**
person specification **17**, 18, **19**
personal circumstances 77
special 80, 95, 129
personality 11, 40, 49, 68, 72, 125
clashes of 129, 143
questions on 130

personality tests **104,** 126
photocopies 97

Prepare (building block) 6, 7, 120
preparing for interview 120–123
presentations 13, 126
  focused 91
  one-minute **40**
probationary period **134–135**
'problem' employees 74
profile 28, 54
  checking and revising **102**
  personal 46
psychometric testing **104**
publications **48,** 54, 65
  trade 30, 113
publicity leaflets **31**

qualifications 11, 15, 17, 47
  professional **39,** 75
  see also academic/educational qualifications
quality 38, **45–49**
questions:
  application form 87, 88
  core 89–91
  interview 8, 120, 122, 123, 124, **127–130, 132** 144–145
  raised in advert 76–77

recession **140–143**
recording/logging **78, 130**
recruitment procedure **20,** 120
recruitment agencies **28**, 34, 100
  adverts from 111
  tips on writing 105
  websites **27**
recruitment managers 34, 48
  adverts 80, 96
  explaining to 115
  face-to-face interviews 125
  loyalty of candidate 79
  pointers from 116
  skim reading 40
redundancy 35, 140
Reed.co.uk 107
  referees/references **49–51,** 53, 54, 134, **143–144**
relocation packages 78
reputation 31, 35, 117
research
  company **31–35,** 112–113, 130
  job **16–21,** 130
  self **8–15**
Research (building block) 6, 7, **38,** 87, **88,** 110
responsibilities 17, 41–44
reward benefits 134
rules 1, 139
  basic 105
  key **88**

salary 13, 15, 76–77, 80, 91, 134, **136**
second opinions 14
senior management CVs **67**
self-help books 15
sequence **52, 80**
signatures 80
skills 9, 12, 31, 101
  additional **75**
  checking by agency 28
  communication 12, 13
  core **10,** 100
  desirable 17, 19
  enhancing your skills **20**, **34, 45, 48, 88**, 141,
  essential 17, 19,87
  extra 54, 129
  'hard' 40, **41–2**
  interviewing 15, 120
  key **73**
  language 47
  level 95
  maintaining 141
  missing **76**
  presentation 12,13
  relevant 121, 129
  'soft' 74
  unqualified 52, 54

Skype **126**
software programs 47, 103, 107, 108
specification
  job 47
  person **17, 19**
speculative applications 105, **110–119**
spelling 81, **98**
staff involvement **48**
strengths and weaknesses 14–15, 32, 105, 130
style **52–3, 54**, **108**
supporting statements 89–91

Target (building block) 6, 10, 87, 88, 97, 110
'tasters' 14
teams 12, 17, 40, 74
technical matters **97–98, 107–108**
telephone 39, **125**
terms and conditions 20, 135
tests **103, 126–127**
time 102, 104
tools of the trade **35–36**
training 13
  courses undertaken at training 13
  work **47**
  opportunities for **10**

troubleshooting **137–145**

using this book **2**

video-conferencing **126**
voluntary work/
volunteering 13, 15, 116, 140, **142**

websites **26–30, 34, 46, 61, 107, 111, 113, 121**
see also online applications

word-processing 35, 68, 98, 103
words 41
buzz 72, 102
key **101,** 102
long or obscure 42
re-use of 75
right 40
work disciolined/fit 129, 140
work history, *see* career history
written English/writing 70
see also handwriting